An excellent practical and no-[...]
develop your own leadership [...]
needing to imitate men in the w[...]
copy as a reminder on how to prepare [...] [...]
conversations and giving copies to the women I know who
are struggling with how to make their way as leaders of the
future. Every capable woman who wants to progress their
career should have a copy. Wish I'd read this 15 years ago!

Sarah Thompson, CEO of St Clare Hospice

This is a must-read for any woman leading today. Carla really
understands what it means to be a woman in the workplace
today. Her empathetic, pragmatic and realistic approach
throughout this guide makes it an invaluable companion
for anyone on their personal and professional development
journey as a leader. A great resource for any female leader
who wants to feel more empowered at work!

Catherine Greenwood, Senior Learning and
Development Specialist, ActionAid UK

A great read – useful, practical and bang on! I wish I'd read
it earlier in my career. I'll be buying it for the established and
emerging leaders I am lucky enough to work with.

Kate Collins, CEO at Teenage Cancer Trust

Carla has created a very special book. Like the friend you
need, when you are having a moment of doubt, the book
comes at the right moment and knows what you are thinking
and gently tells you how to help yourself move on. If you
have even experienced self-doubt (ehmm all of us!) then this
book will leave you feeling like you can take on that doubt

and knock it out. I felt very uplifted and hopeful, and reassured that it's not just me that sometimes has these doubting thoughts. Carla has created a brilliant guide to navigate through life, not just work!

Eleanor Tweddell, author of *Why Losing Your Job Could be the Best Thing That Ever Happened to You*

An empowering, practical and at times a window into the soul of the female leader guide. Whether you read it in one go or take bite-size sections as you need it, this book is a must-have for your leadership journey.

Lindsay Fyffe-Jardine, CEO

This is the leadership book we've been waiting for – the perfect combination of practical advice, tools and guidance. It's the ideal guide for those at the top, those aiming for the top and those starting their journey.

Donna Holland, CEO at Rockinghorse Children's Charity

Closing the Influence Gap provides such a practical, thoughtful and well-rounded guide for women who know they have more to offer and want to break through. Carla's experience coaching female leaders shines through, as does her wisdom and empathy.

Harriet Minter, author of *WFH: How to Build a Career You Love When You're Not in the Office*

A must-read for any female leaders who want to have more impact in their work and improve their relationship with themself and others. This book is practical yet powerful and is laid out in a way that you can dip in and out – accessing useful techniques to help you overcome whatever gremlins may be keeping your potential locked up.

Lizzie Martin, Leadership Coach and Founder of Work Life Mother

A must-read for those seeking to silence feelings of imposter syndrome to unleash their true potential. This book leaves you feeling truly empowered and equipped to take on the challenges of leadership. After reading this, you realise you are capable of it all. A book to revisit again and again.

Rachel Maguire and Hannah Hall-Turner, @thejobsharepair

This new guide for women leaders will give you valuable insight and practical tips whether you're starting out in your leadership journey or have been in senior roles for years. Drawing on her considerable experience as a coach and leader, Carla has written an engaging guide to help you lead and influence more successfully. It's full of useful exercises and stories to bring key points to life as well as lots of reassurance that you're not alone, and the conversational and easy to read style makes it feel like having a coach by your side in written form. A really good addition to your leadership tool kit.

Kath Abrahams, CEO at Tommy's

This thoughtfully written self-help guide is the resource that women leaders are searching for. It emphasises that women don't need to fix themselves to fit into environments designed for men, and they can unleash their leadership ability by diminishing the systemic negative influences surrounding them that often hold women back from fulfilling their potential. With practical solutions and coaching tools, it explains how to successfully navigate the workplace and tackle gender bias with proven strategies that work. Carla's voice speaks as a reassuring and encouraging mentor through the pages of the book, reminding the reader that they are not alone in this journey and providing support every step of the way.

Julia Muir, Founder of Automotive 30% Club and author of *Change the Game*

What I loved about this book is how practical and topical it is. Carla has done a great job at creating a companion that will always be there for aspiring and existing women leaders, guiding them through their career path. Full of practical advice and coaching technique tools, this is the book I wish I had been given at the start of my own career.

Mylene Sylvestre, Publishing Director, *The Guardian*

Closing the Influence Gap

A practical guide for women leaders who want to be heard

Carla Miller

First published in Great Britain by Practical Inspiration Publishing, 2022

ISBN   9781788603614   (print)
       9781788603638   (epub)
       9781788603621   (mobi)

Want to bulk-buy copies of this book for your team and colleagues? We can introduce case studies, customize the content and co-brand *Closing the Influence Gap* to suit your business's needs.

Please email info@practicalinspiration.com for more details.

Practical Inspiration Publishing

Contents

Your Coaching Toolkit

Within this book you'll find a series of coaching tools that
you can use to show up as an influential and confident
leader at work.

Introduction

The extent of the Influence Gap

Women leaders across the globe are experiencing the Influence Gap and this is a systemic problem, not a problem with women.

We hold fewer positions of power and so it is hard for us to get a seat at the table for the discussions and decisions that matter. As of 2022, women hold only 29% of senior management roles globally[1] despite the fact that gender diversity is known to improve profitability.[2] In 2021, only 8% of Fortune 500 CEOs were women and half of start-ups had no women on their leadership teams.[3] Progress has been set back by the COVID-19 pandemic, during which LinkedIn saw a marked decline in the hiring of women into leadership roles.[4]

Our leadership skills are equal to those of men yet we are less likely to be encouraged into a leadership role.[5] Men are twice as likely to be promoted or selected for leadership training,[6] while a study published in *The Leadership Quarterly* showed that "Men were encouraged to step forward and 'claim their space' as leaders and women were advised to take a narrower focus by developing specific areas of expertise and appeasing colleagues."[7] Men tend to be more confident about their leadership skills, rating themselves as better leaders than women do but in fact other people often rate female managers more highly for leadership effectiveness.[8]

We can be judged for stepping into our authority. An article in the *Harvard Business Review* on the unseen barriers to women rising into leadership roles shared that "Integrating leadership into one's core identity is particularly challenging for women, who must establish credibility in a culture that is deeply conflicted about whether, when, and how they should exercise authority."[9]

We struggle to get our voices heard in meetings. It's not just about getting a seat at the table – we need to be heard when we get there. Research conducted by RADA in Business found that only 8% of women find it easy to make their voice heard in the workplace and women are 12% more likely than men to feel uncomfortable when meeting with board members or senior management.[10] Victoria Brescoll found in her research that women are given lower competence ratings than men when they are vocal in meetings[11] even though men were found to speak more often and for longer.[12]

We are trying to succeed in a working culture that was designed for men, by men and as a result only one in five women feel a strong sense of belonging in the workplace. This makes it harder for us to share dissenting views.[13]

According to the McKinsey & Company *Women in the Workplace 2020* report:

> Senior-level women are also nearly twice as likely as women overall to be "Onlys"—the only or one of the only women in the room at work. That comes with its own challenges: women who are Onlys are more likely than women who work with other women to feel pressure to work more and to experience

microaggressions, including needing to provide additional evidence of their competence.[14]

Women of color are often an "Only" in two ways and are even more likely to be on the other end of disrespectful behavior.[15]

It's no wonder so many talented women experience imposter feelings! I truly believe that women are experiencing significant imposter feelings because of the environment we are working within and that sense that we don't belong. When we try and replicate the behavior of our male colleagues it feels awkward and we are criticized for it, but when we conform to society's expectations of how women should act, we often go unheard and unrewarded.

The purpose of this book

This book aims to empower you as a woman to successfully navigate the workplace and tackle gender bias using proven strategies that work. In the coming chapters you'll learn how to reduce self-doubt, confidently lead your way and influence upwards. We are going to get your voice heard!

You are going to take so much from this book in the form of practical strategies, insights and tools that you can use on a daily basis to empower you in your role and increase your influence. But there are two things I hope you will *feel* while you read this book:

1. You are not alone

You are not alone in your self-doubt, in your worry or imposter feelings or in the challenges you face. The other women that you look at in meetings and you think have it all sorted – behind the confident exterior, they share many of the same thoughts, feelings and challenges as you do. I know this because I have now brought together thousands of women at all levels through my workshops and coaching programs and when I give them a safe space to share, they open up to each other and realize that they are experiencing a shared struggle.

2. There is nothing wrong with you

You do not need fixing. It is not your fault that your voice isn't being heard. The evidence I've shared above should reassure you that there is a systemic problem with how women are perceived in the workplace, not a problem with you.

How the book works

Part 1 of this book will help you to tackle any self-doubt and imposter feelings you may have and help you to believe in yourself. This first step of seeing yourself as a leader is crucial.

Then Part 2 will make sure others see you as a leader. You'll be creating your Personal Leadership Brand, and learning how to stop giving your power away and step into the authority that comes with your role.

In Part 3, you'll be developing the advanced influencing skills that will enable you to successfully navigate internal politics and speak with confidence and clarity to senior stakeholders, thereby increasing your influence and impact.

In Part 4, I'll be encouraging you to take control of your career, helping you to prepare for each stage of your leadership journey and to increase your visibility.

And finally, I've included a Troubleshooting section in Part 5, where I share answers to the very honest and vulnerable questions that the women leaders in my Influence & Impact course have asked me. In the workplace it is often hard to talk about these topics and you may well be asking the same questions. You'll see these questions signposted in relevant chapters. You also get access to my online portal at www.carlamillertraining.com/bookresources where you'll find the bonus resources referred to in the book.

We rise together

It would be remiss not to acknowledge that the workplace is unequal in many ways beyond gender and we will only see real progress when inequality is unacceptable and diversity is truly embraced. My particular focus is on gender inequality but I'm very conscious that I write this book as someone who has personally faced fewer barriers to success than many other women, by nature of my background and race. I want to acknowledge that many women struggle to speak up and be heard because of forms of discrimination such as racism, homophobia, ableism, transphobia, classism and sexual harassment that go beyond the unconscious gender bias I refer to in this book. If that is your experience, I encourage you to trust your own judgment when applying the techniques in this book. Read this book knowing that it applies when you are working with reasonable people in a healthy working environment. If something doesn't feel like a safe thing to do in your environment or given past experiences, please don't do it. Take what works for you; ignore what doesn't.

In the book, I draw on my own experiences but also those of my clients, including hundreds of women who have gone through my Influence & Impact course. It's a group which is diverse in many ways, from sectors and job titles to ethnicity, neurodiversity, age and education, and they have each used what you will learn here to increase their influence in their existing roles, secure promotions and move to new jobs. I've shared their stories while changing names and details to protect their confidentiality.

My hope is that the content proves valuable to any woman reading and that as a reader you will use the influence that this book will help you to build to support, encourage and empower your colleagues who face barriers to their success in the workplace due to systemic inequality.

Take others with you as you rise − that is true leadership in my mind.

I have been on this journey with hundreds of women in my Influence & Impact course and I can't wait to go on it with you. So let's get started...

Part 1

Seeing yourself as a leader

Most books about influencing are focused on strategies, tactics and tools. And you will find plenty of those within the covers of this book, but becoming an influential leader starts with seeing yourself as a leader. I call this the inner work of leadership.

In Part 1 you'll be learning powerful new coaching tools that you can use on a daily basis to boost your confidence and self-belief. You'll feel less alone as we explore why we all feel like an imposter sometimes. You'll understand how you can stop seeking validation from others and instead find it within yourself. And you'll be able to receive negative feedback without going into a spiral of self-doubt and imposter feelings.

In short, you will start to see yourself as the influential and inspiring leader that you are.

Chapter 1 – Tackling self-doubt

When you can quieten your negative self-talk and start trusting your own judgment, self-doubt will become occasional rather than constant.

Chapter 2 – Mastering your mindset

By leaving behind any unhelpful habits such as perfectionism, overworking and worry, you'll free up mental space for the things you actually want to focus on!

Chapter 3 – Dealing with the tough days

We all have tough days and this chapter will help you handle overwhelm, avoid burnout and handle negative feedback with grace.

Chapter 1

Tackling self-doubt

Self-doubt is one of the main themes that comes up when I coach women leaders, regardless of how successful or established they are. It can stop you speaking up, make you question your own judgment and hold you back in your career. So let's explore where self-doubt and imposter feelings come from and what you can do to quieten them.

Tackling imposter feelings

You've no doubt heard of imposter syndrome, a concept that originated in a 1978 paper by Dr Pauline Clance and Dr Suzanne Imes called "The imposter phenomenon in high-achieving women: Dynamics and therapeutic interventions."[1] As psychologists at Georgia State University they observed that many of their high-performing female students shared in counseling sessions that they felt their success was undeserved. Now, the term is associated with a fear of being "found out" or discovered as a "fraud" that comes up regardless of how successful and capable you are.

I'm not a fan of labeling yourself as having a syndrome so I prefer to talk about imposter feelings and the wider spectrum of self-doubt within which they sit.

Some of us experience constant self-doubt like Jo, a project manager in Financial Services, who was always comparing herself negatively to others and worried that she was going to be fired. She was actually really good at her job and received great feedback from her manager, but she couldn't believe it because all she could see were her faults.

Others experience a surge of self-doubt when they are outside of their comfort zone – perhaps due to a promotion, a new line manager or a challenging time at work. For my coaching client Laura, who led an account management team in an ad agency, it came up when she became a director and suddenly felt out of her depth. She was worried everyone would think that her boss had made a mistake giving her the job.

Self-doubt can sound like:

"I got lucky."

"Someone else could do my job better than me."

"They must have made a mistake."

"If I can do it, it's not that hard."

"They're just saying that because they like me."

"I should be more like that person."

"I need more experience/qualifications/gravitas before I'm good enough for that role."

"I'm finding this hard; I must be failing in my role."

"I did so well at interview, now they'll expect me to be better than I am."

"They think I know more than I actually do – I'm going to disappoint."

When women join my Influence & Impact course they share with others in the group what has prompted them to join. Many of them share the self-doubt and imposter feelings they experience and at least one person will say that they feel less alone after hearing from others. So often we compare our insides to others' outsides. We know that we experience self-doubt, imposter feelings, comparison and insecurity but we assume that everyone else feels as confident on the inside as they appear on the outside. Being part of a community of women where you can share honestly and safely helps disavow that myth.

> *"I thought my Inner Critic was abnormally loud and all the women around me were much more confident than me. It was such a relief to know that how I feel is totally normal." Ava*

I also believe that the workplace culture in which we operate exacerbates self-doubt and imposter feelings for many women. When we struggle to get our voices heard, or when men receive credit for making the point we just made, it can be easy to interpret that as a personal shortcoming, when in fact it is a systemic problem. *Women are still trying to prove themselves in a workplace designed by men, for men and that is bound to have an impact on our confidence and self-belief.*

My goal is that through using the Inner Critic and Inner Leader coaching tools in this section, you, like my coaching clients Laura and Jo, will start to experience less self-doubt and much more self-belief.

Coaching tool: Turning down the volume on your Inner Critic

We all have self-doubt because we all have an Inner Critic. Learning how to turn down the volume on your Inner Critic is the most powerful step you can take toward believing in yourself. And when you believe in yourself, others will too. In this chapter, I'm going to share the steps you can take to quieten your negative mental chatter and make your head a happier place to be.

What is an Inner Critic?

Have you noticed that you speak more harshly to yourself then you ever would to anyone else? We have many thousands of thoughts each day, the vast majority of which are repetitive and a fair few of those will be negative.

Your Inner Critic can sound like:

"I can't believe I made such a stupid mistake – what an idiot!"
"I'm such a failure."
"I'm not good/intelligent/likeable/loveable enough."
"There's something wrong with me."
"Everyone thinks that piece of work I did is rubbish."
"That was a stupid thing to say and everyone is judging me for it."

In coaching we refer to this negative self-talk as your Inner Critic because it is a running commentary of all the things you've done wrong and the ways in which you should be better. Our Inner Critic tells us that we're not good enough and we will never be good enough. It thinks it can mind read what others think of us (it can't) and it likes to think it can predict the future too, always focusing on the worst-case scenario.

When I speak to women on coaching calls, they will often tell me that their Inner Critic is super loud and they think that means there is something wrong with them. If that resonates with you, you can stop judging yourself now because we *all* have an Inner Critic (yes, even us coaches) – it is just part of being human.

There is a part of our brains called the amygdala which is constantly on the lookout for threats and danger. This is where the fight, flight or freeze instinct comes from, which evolved in times when human lives were in constant physical danger and its role was to keep us safe. Sounds good, right?

Unfortunately, it thinks everything that takes us away from the safe and the known is a danger. That opportunity for a promotion – dangerous! Speaking up in a big meeting – dangerous! Asking someone to mentor you – dangerous!

Going right back to your early childhood, if you've tried something before and it led to failure, rejection, shame, abandonment, hurt or disappointment then your Inner Critic adds it to the list of things to avoid. Our Inner Critic can always make a persuasive argument, which if we believe it will keep us playing it small and safe.

Steps to turn down the volume on your Inner Critic

I can't teach you how to completely silence your Inner Critic and I wouldn't want to. That part of your brain exists for a reason and there could be times of genuine danger when you need to fight, take flight or freeze. *But* you don't want it to be in charge when you are making decisions, or to be chattering away all day making you feel bad about yourself. So here are the steps to take to help you turn down the volume on your Inner Critic:

1. Accept your Inner Critic – think of it as a well-meaning but misguided part of yourself that is trying to keep you safe. You could even simplify your Inner Critic by calling it fear – and feeling fear is part of the human experience. Having an Inner Critic doesn't mean you are broken or need fixing. You can treat your Inner Critic (and yourself) with kindness rather than judgment.

2. Drop the idea that all your thoughts are true – just because you think something, it doesn't mean it is true. Your thoughts are all made-up stories based on your experience, your view of the world, your hopes and your fears. That's a mind-blowing idea but a crucial one so I'm going to repeat it for you. *Just because you think something, it doesn't mean it is true.* So, if your thoughts are all made-up stories then you can choose to stop believing the ones that make you feel bad. Yes, it really can be that simple.

3. Notice your Inner Critic – start by paying more atten-tion to your mental chatter. You can notice when you

are being unkind to yourself and recognize it as your Inner Critic.

4. Give your Inner Critic a personality – currently you probably hear your critical thoughts in your own voice, which can make them feel more true. By personifying your Inner Critic we can make your negative self-talk stand out from the rest of your thoughts, creating a bit of space for you to question its validity. You can choose one or all of the options below to personify your Inner Critic...

   ▪ *You can give your Inner Critic a name* – something that sums it up and sounds ridiculous. I've heard names like Doubting Debbie, Cautious Clara, Nervous Nancy, Critical Cora, Worrying Wanda. Clients have also picked names of mean girls they went to school with or harsh teachers they had. Some people have one Inner Critic personality, while others have multiple Inner Critic personalities – there are no rules here, just do what feels right to you.

   ▪ *You can visualize your Inner Critic* – what does it look like? Is it a person, creature or object? Can you draw it? I've had clients visualize their Inner Critic as a person, a creature, an object like a net or an image like a shadow. My one piece of advice on this is don't make it terrifying – the point of personifying it is to help diminish its strength not increase it!

▪ *You can give your Inner Critic a voice.* It could be a booming voice, a whisper, a high-pitched or squeaky voice, for example.

Some people find it easier than others to personify their Inner Critic. If you find personifying it hard then you can stick to calling it your Inner Critic or calling it fear.

5. Thank and dismiss it – when your Inner Critic gets vocal you can recognize it, thank it for the input and dismiss it. "Thanks, but I've got this" works perfectly for me and I imagine putting my hand up in a "talk to the hand" gesture.

Alternatively, you could imagine it getting smaller and smaller until it is so tiny you can't see it. Or getting quieter and quieter until you can't hear it. The more ridiculous the better, as it reduces the power of its words.

"I used to be too anxious to speak up in meetings for fear of saying something stupid and then I'd get annoyed when someone else raised the idea I had. Now I can recognize when Mean Miranda is getting vocal and imagine turning down her volume. I can speak up in meetings without feeling anxious and I've been getting good feedback from my CEO as a result." Alex

My favorite metaphor for this process comes from Elizabeth Gilbert in her brilliant book *Big Magic*. She shares that whenever she writes a book, she thinks of it as going on a road trip. Creativity is always right next to her in the passenger seat and she accepts that Fear is always going to be along for the ride too. She says to Fear that they are welcome to come along but no backseat driving:

You're not allowed to touch the road maps, you're not allowed to suggest detours, you're not allowed to fiddle with the temperature. Dude, you're not even allowed to touch the radio. But above all else, my dear old familiar friend, you are absolutely forbidden to drive.[2]

What next?

Quietening your Inner Critic isn't a "one and done" thing. It is an ongoing process – it will often be trying to be a backseat driver in your car. Your Inner Critic, along with its mates self-doubt and imposter feelings, will step up its activity when you are outside of your comfort zone. Now you can recognize that as a normal reaction to new and unknown situations.

You can also notice what situations cause your Inner Critic to be more vocal and be proactive about reducing its impact, for example by imagining leaving it at the door of a challenging meeting rather than taking it in with you.

There is one other secret to turning down the volume on your Inner Critic and it's something you probably weren't expecting to read in a leadership book. My experience is that the more I love myself, the less vocal my Inner Critic is. I'm not sure I even liked myself very much as a teenager and my Inner Critic dominated my thoughts. As I've got older I have learned to get better at appreciating my uniqueness, accepting and embracing my imperfections, and treating myself with kindness and compassion.

My best piece of advice to anyone who has a vocal Inner Critic is to get better at loving yourself, to the point where you recognize that you are actually amazing exactly as you are, flaws and all. I've shared some tips on how to do this in Chapter 3.

Coaching tool: Tuning in to your Inner Leader

The good news is that as well as an Inner Critic, you have an Inner Leader. Your Inner Leader is the calm, wise, confident part of you that always knows the best thing to do in any situation. Think of her as your inner wisdom or as a personification of your intuition. You may have channeled your Inner Leader at various points during your career without realizing it – usually in moments when you feel like you have everything under control and know you are good at what you do.

Unfortunately, we are usually more tuned into our Inner Critic than our Inner Leader. We want to change that today so that you can proactively tune in to your Inner Leader whenever you need her.

Getting to know your Inner Leader

I've recorded a visualization for you, inspired by the visualization I learned from the Coaches Training Institute, which will help you connect with your Inner Leader. Head on over to the online book resources at www.carlamillertraining.com/bookresources to listen to that.

If you can't listen to the visualization right now there are a couple of shortcuts to tapping into a powerful and wise version of you:

- **Tune in to your intuition** – close your eyes, take a few deep breaths and feel your feet on the floor. Then place your hand on your heart and ask yourself *"What do I need to know?"*
- **Use your body language** to go into situations feeling powerful – stand up straight, shoulders back, head held high and you will feel more empowered (more on this in Chapter 5). This is how it feels to embody your Inner Leader and you can shift into feeling empowered by adopting that body language.
- **Re-live a moment when you felt confident and wise.** Perhaps you were doing work you loved, or perhaps you received some great feedback and thought *"I'm doing a really good job."* Think of that moment and then replay it in slow motion in your mind – what were you feeling, what were you thinking to yourself? Turn up the intensity of those feelings until you are feeling really good.

Working with your Inner Leader

Here's how you can use your Inner Leader to help you on a daily basis:

- Connect with your Inner Leader before a challenging meeting or call so that when you are going into that situation you are embodying your Inner Leader.
- Tune in to your Inner Leader when you notice yourself feeling overwhelmed or confused.
- Connect with your Inner Leader when you need your mojo back or you need wisdom. I connect with my Inner Leader before every coaching call to help me feel grounded and also before anything where I might be nervous, such as a pitch or talking to a new client.

"The Inner Leader I met in the visualization is a warrior goddess! I pictured her in my mind whilst I waited backstage ahead of a big presentation this week and I felt so powerful walking onto the stage instead of my usual nerves." Kerrie

We often look to others for advice, but you have access to an internal wealth of wisdom about what is right for you and what the right thing to do is in any situation. Now you know how to tune in to it.

Validating yourself

Do you feel like you're not doing a good job unless someone tells you that you are? Are you always wanting more feedback and praise than your manager provides? Do you need a lot of reassurance to feel happy with your performance? If any of these resonate, then the likelihood is that you're seeking validation from others rather than getting it from yourself. Let's talk about how that's holding you back and what you can do about it.

I noticed a surge of imposter feelings popping up for my clients during the various lockdowns engendered by the COVID-19 pandemic when many people were working remotely. Our everyday interactions in-person with our colleagues send us reassuring signals that everything is okay. A comment or a question delivered with a smile can remove tension. We can chat socially to a colleague as we leave the room after a difficult meeting, which also releases the tension. Working virtually has become common and has many upsides but it gives us less opportunities to connect informally. Without that unspoken reassurance, we can experience a vacuum, and nature hates a vacuum so often our Inner Critic steps in to fill it. But this isn't just related to working remotely; it crops up all the time.

"I feel like I need my mentor to constantly tell me I'm doing a great job. When I don't get that feedback, I find myself being self-deprecating in the hope he will contradict me. I can sense he's getting frustrated with me fishing for compliments, but I can't stop." Mia

This affects a lot of us. Elizabeth Thornton, author of *The Objective Leader*, talks about a study she ran where 55% of people said that their self-worth was *often, more often* or *always* tied to what others think of them.[3]

This can be particularly prevalent among high achievers according to Dr Risa Stein, Professor of Psychology at Rockhurst University, who says, "One false step and they [high achievers] lose that external validation and those rewards, and then there goes their sense of identity and who they are. And then without those rewards... they question their self-worth, and that's real damaging."[4]

Many of us learned that when we came home from school with a great exam result or we won something, then we got praised. And that positive attention can feel like love. So we decide that how loveable we are is directly related to how successful we are. This need for validation is a completely natural response to the situations we found ourselves in as children.

It feels nice to have that feedback and reassurance. But for some of us, we rely on it to know our own worth. And that's not so healthy for several reasons.

If external validation is not just a *nice* to have, but a *need* to have, then we don't feel safe disagreeing with others or challenging others because then they won't approve of us. And that will mean something about our value as a person.

If you really relate to the idea of being a people pleaser, it can be hard to know what you really want and what you really need, because you are more guided by how others will react. I am by nature a big people pleaser. I used to edit what I said based on the reaction I thought it was going to get. That can be an emotionally intelligent thing to do, but then it got to the point where I edited so much that I would never even think about what I wanted from a situation. I would be so focused on the potential reaction that my brain would just skip over the bit of what I wanted and go straight to *"what's going to get the best reaction here?"*.

Seeking constant feedback and reassurance from our managers can get quite annoying for them. They have bigger priorities on their to-do list than boosting our egos. Plus the more senior you get, the less time that your manager has for you and once you get to chief executive level, you've got no-one above you, which makes it much harder to get that feedback and reassurance. You have to be able to give it to yourself in order to stay mentally healthy at that level. So if you are looking to become more senior, this is one of the habits you'll want to kick.

If you are constantly needing reassurance from others, then you are constantly vulnerable to the external world for your self-worth and your happiness. *You are always giving your power away and hoping that people will then give it back to you.* And our Inner Critic and imposter feelings can get really out of control when we don't get that feedback. If we suddenly have a manager that isn't great at reassuring us and giving feedback, or if we're having a difficult time or in the wrong job and not able to perform, then our Inner Critic gets very loud.

All because we've attached a lot of our worth to what other people say about us and what they tell us.

In fact, we never really know what someone else thinks of us. We're basically making it up based on what we *think* other people think about us, as we're not mind readers. And most of the time we get it wrong because it's our Inner Critic talking.

There's an idea from Buddhism about the hungry ghost. A hungry ghost is when, however much feedback, reassurance and validation we get from others, it is never enough. We never actually feel truly satisfied. Our Inner Critic can always discredit the positive things they say.

The only validation that really matters, and that fills that hole inside you, that feeds that hungry ghost, doesn't come from other people. It comes from you.

If you're not practiced at giving yourself validation or if you've got no idea how to give yourself validation, then the idea that it doesn't come from others might be quite unsettling. But as author Louise Hay says, "You've been criticizing yourself for years, and it hasn't worked. Try approving of yourself and see what happens."[5]

How do we start to give ourselves validation instead of constantly looking to others?

1. Start by looking at your beliefs. You can use the reframing beliefs coaching tool in the next chapter to work with any unhelpful beliefs you may have such as *"I need to be successful in order to be loveable"* or *"My value as a person is attached to what others say about me."* That tool will enable you to create and embed new beliefs such as *"I am enough exactly as I am,"* so that you can

start feeling safe without needing reassurance from others.

2. Get to know your needs. If you think you might be a people pleaser who is more in tune with the needs of others than your own needs, it's time for you to start getting to know yourself and getting more grounded in who you are. You could do some journaling, or go for a long walk and ask yourself:

> *"What do I like?"*
> *"What do I want?"*
> *"What do I need right now?"*

Your answers to those questions will help you tune in to your own needs, making it easier to consider those alongside the needs of others.

3. Learn how to validate yourself. That's about learning to really like and recognize the great things about yourself and a lot of people find this uncomfortable to do. You can start writing a list of things you like about yourself. It could be that you're really kind. It could be that you're really loyal. It could be that you like the way that your brain thinks. If you're trying to validate yourself within your role, think of the things that you are good at within your role, because I suspect you've been focused on the things you don't feel so good at. And if you're keeping a gratitude diary, include something about yourself that you feel grateful for. It's brilliant to be grateful for everything else that's going on around you but be grateful for something about yourself; give yourself some recognition.

4. Tell yourself what you really need to hear. What do you hope someone else will tell you? What validation is it that you want from them? Then give that to yourself. Give yourself the praise you hoped you'd get from your manager. Tell yourself you're doing a good job.

 How do I deal with professional jealousy?
See page 209.

Chapter 1: Top tips

- Give your Inner Critic a personality so you can recognize when it is speaking.

- When you notice your Inner Critic cropping up, thank and dismiss it rather than let it stay in the driving seat of your mind.

- Tune in to your Inner Leader before you go into a challenging situation or when you want to feel more confident.

- Notice when you are asking others for validation and try and give yourself that validation instead.

- Add something you like about yourself to your daily gratitude practice.

Chapter 2

Mastering your mindset

Imposter feelings crop up because many of us feel we have to be perfect at work, so when we make a mistake we start to question our worthiness for the role. In this chapter we are going to explore how perfectionism may be hindering you more than it is helping you. We'll also be learning how to deal with those work worries that stop you falling asleep or wake you up at 2am.

Saying goodbye to perfectionism and overworking

For years I thought that I was doing well in my career *because* I worked so hard and held myself to such high standards. It took working with a coach to help me realize that those strategies were causing me as much harm as they were good.

Yes, I was getting great results. But overworking and perfectionism were causing me to exhaust myself and to emotionally overinvest in work to the point where I took everything personally. My identity had become so entwined with my work and performance that I didn't really know who I was without my job title. I was stressed out, trying to control things that were out of my control and unable to gain perspective on challenging situations.

My coach asked me two questions that challenged my thinking and I'd like to share those questions with you now:

What would happen if you didn't try and be perfect at everything?

What would happen if you didn't give 110% all the time?

When I first heard those questions, I almost hyperventilated at the idea of not trying to be perfect or give 110%. I thought to myself, *"Why would you not want to be perfect or as good as you possibly can be? Why would you not want to give your all, all the time?"*

But when I reflected, I realized that the reason I was trying to be perfect was to feel good enough. And the reason I gave 110% was to prove to myself and everyone else that I deserved to be there.

I had never articulated it to myself before that moment, but at a subconscious level **I believed that the quality of my work was directly linked to my value as a person**.

I've now worked with hundreds of women that share this belief. Perhaps it rings true for you too? If so, I want you to read the next few lines over and over again until they really sink in…

You are good enough. In fact, you are more than good enough – you are amazing, exactly as you are. Your worth is innate. Yes, with all your imperfections. Your imperfections are part of the uniqueness of who you are.

You don't have to prove anything to anyone. Your worth is not determined by the quality of your work, how hard you work or what others think of you.

When we try and be perfect, we fear being seen as we really are. But to make genuine connections with people, to be loved for who we are, we need to *show* people who we really are. That is as relevant in work and leadership as it is in personal relationships. We want leaders who are relatable and human, who understand when we make mistakes because they've also made their own fair share of mistakes.

Perfectionism isn't the same as a healthy drive for excellence. It is entirely possible to set yourself high standards, get excited by big goals, and perform well without the tyranny of perfectionism and overworking. Perfectionism is when your standards are unreachable, when you can't enjoy the journey because you are so focused on the goal and when failure means something negative about you and is hard to bounce back from.

Now you're on board with the idea that perfectionism may be more of an enemy to your career than a friend, what can you do about it? How do you break the habit of a lifetime of overdelivering?

1. Consciously choose your effort level

If perfectionism is something you experience, then in all likelihood you're applying your full energy to absolutely everything that you take on. Sounds admirable, especially for those of us who had a strong work ethic ingrained in us young. But actually, it's a poor use of resources and a sure-fire way to burn out.

Don't believe me? Look at your to-do list. Look at how many things are on it. Now work out how long you'd need to allocate to each task to do it to the absolute best of your ability. When you add those hours up, I'd be astounded if they did not vastly exceed your working hours. It simply isn't possible to do everything on your to-do list to the best of your ability and still meet deadlines, attend meetings and read all your emails. And when that to-do list builds up it stops you taking on the interesting projects that could advance your career.

Not everything *requires* your full energy and effort. If you're working on a detailed budget forecast, then, absolutely, you want it to be completely accurate and need to take the time to get it right. But if you're sending an email to a colleague, then a typo isn't the end of the world. You probably don't need to reread it five times to check that it's okay; you can just give it a quick once-over and send it.

The skill is in consciously and strategically choosing your effort level. Look at your to-do list and start identifying some tasks that don't require you to give 10 out of 10 effort. Sometimes a task is an 8 out of 10. Or sometimes it's even a 6 out of 10. In any one day, you ideally have a mixture of effort level in terms of tasks, so that your brain gets a chance to rest a bit between the high-effort tasks.

2. Don't get stuck in fifth gear

When you drive a car you don't just stick it in the highest gear and stay there regardless of the road and traffic. Cars aren't designed to be constantly driven in fifth gear. Guess what – neither are you! My default for so long was to be in fifth gear – always pushing myself harder and harder in the hope of feeling like I was good enough and adding enough value. My engine basically broke down, as I share in Chapter 3. If you're in a senior role you need to think of it as a marathon, not a sprint, and pace yourself accordingly or you'll have collapsed long before you reach the finish line.

3. Recalibrate your standards

Have I mentioned that it's challenging working for a perfectionist? You're constantly trying to meet standards that you can't quite picture and feeling like you've disappointed someone even when you've done a good job.

If you are highly driven, then your version of good might well be someone else's version of excellence. You may be constantly going above and beyond unnecessarily, creating more work for other people. Those super-high standards that you're holding yourself and other people to could be holding the team back, because other people feel like they can't meet them.

4. Done is better than perfect

Perfectionism often goes hand in hand with procrastination. The idea of starting something can be overwhelming if you think it needs to be perfect and so you delay starting. Or you delay submitting a piece of work because you are constantly improving it and it never feels perfect enough to submit. Procrastination and missing deadlines will damage your reputation much more than submitting a piece of work that is good, as opposed to perfect.

Try and make peace with the fact that done is better than perfect and that in many situations good is good enough; it doesn't need to be absolutely perfect. You can give yourself permission to do great but imperfect work if precision isn't called for.

5. Practice embracing failure

Try adopting what Dr Carol Dweck calls a growth mindset, where failure doesn't mean anything about you as a person; instead, it is useful information that you can use to learn and grow.[1] We'll talk about this more in the next chapter. I practiced embracing failure by taking up tennis, a hobby that I enjoyed but wasn't particularly good at. At first, I was constantly apologizing for poor shots and getting frustrated with myself. Then I decided to enjoy learning and to embrace the fact that it was going to take me thousands of poor shots before I had played enough to have consistent good shots. Now I have a decent backhand and serve.

6. Check in with yourself

Start by noticing the physical signs that you are feeling stressed or in overdrive. Then gift yourself some space to reflect on what belief is driving your behavior. Using the coaching tool I'm about to share will help you to reframe that belief into one that encourages you to healthily strive toward excellence rather than constantly needing to prove your value.

These techniques work. Corinna came to me for coaching as she was tired of working so hard yet never feeling satisfied with her progress.

"I hadn't realized how hard I was being on myself trying to make everything perfect, or the impact it was having on my team. I've been using the effort level technique with my team and they love it. 'Good is good enough' is my new mantra and it has allowed me to stop working every evening and leave on time to meet friends or go to the gym. It's great to be enjoying work and the rest of my life more." Corinna

This next tool I'm going to share with you is really powerful for changing unhelpful thought patterns like perfectionism and self-doubt.

 ## Coaching tool: Reframing your unhelpful beliefs

As we go through life, we build up our model of the world based on our experiences. This starts very young. As babies we learn that when we smile we get a positive response from our caregivers, so we smile more. As children we are like little sponges absorbing everything around us and making sense of it in our heads. If you are shouted at for being loud and that upsets you, then you learn that it isn't safe to speak up. If you are laughed at by other kids for making a mistake, you learn that making mistakes creates shame and isn't a safe thing to do. If you get rebuked for things you did by accident, you learn that you need to edit and control everything you do and say in order to avoid criticism and feel safe.

Our brain likes shortcuts, so it creates these generalizations about life, which in coaching we call beliefs. Despite forming many of these beliefs when we are young, we never question them. We carry them with us into adulthood and let them continue to shape our view of the world and therefore our behavior. Inevitably, some of these beliefs are unhelpful.

We hold unhelpful beliefs about ourselves and our abilities, about relationships, work and life in general. And these beliefs don't sit harmlessly in our heads; we play them out daily. Beliefs like:

"It isn't safe to make mistakes," which means we triple-check everything and beat ourselves up for even tiny mistakes.

"I must remain in control at all times," which makes it hard to delegate and empower our teams.

"I'm not good enough," which makes us overwork to try and prove ourselves.

"Asking for help is a sign of weakness," which leads to burnout.

"I need to be perfect to prove I deserve to be here," which make us anxious.

"I must always have the right answer," which makes it challenging to manage people who know more about their area than we do.

"To be successful you have to be X," which stops us applying for promotions.

Our beliefs determine the actions we take and the actions we take determine the results we get.

If you believe that an employer will never give a director job to someone your age, then you don't apply and you have zero chance of getting that job.

If you believe that your organization isn't open to change, then you don't bother suggesting new ways of doing things and nothing changes.

If you believe that your manager doesn't listen to you, then you don't speak up so they have no idea what you think, or you become resentful and the relationship becomes tense.

Reframing your unhelpful beliefs

If you accept that you've probably got a few unhelpful beliefs lurking around in your head, what can you do about that? Here is a simple approach you can use.

1. Notice the feeling
2. Identify the belief
3. Question and reframe the belief
4. Embed your new belief

1. Notice the feeling

If you're having a thought that makes you feel bad about yourself, are experiencing a negative emotion or feeling negative about the future, it is likely fueled by an unhelpful belief. Noticing the feeling is the first step to spotting that you have an unhelpful belief.

2. Identify the belief

What is the thought that is causing that negative feeling? What were you saying to yourself as those emotions popped up? Explore this until you land on the thought that pours the most fuel on the fire of the negative feelings. That is your belief. It might appear to be specific to that situation, e.g., "X didn't listen to me," but if you delve a bit deeper it could actually be a more generic belief such as "X never listens to me" or "No-one cares what I have to say" or "My opinion isn't valued in this organization."

3. Question and reframe the belief

In her book *Loving What Is*, Byron Katie suggests some powerful questions to help you create some chinks in the armor of your unhelpful beliefs.[2] The questions below are an adaptation of these that you can apply to your unhelpful thought or belief.

- Is it true?
- Is it 100% true in all situations or can you think of a time when it wasn't true?
- How do you feel when you think that thought?
- How does it make you act?
- Who would you be without that thought?
- How do you want to feel?
- What would you need to believe to feel the way you want to feel?
- What belief would you like to have going forward?

Here's an example of what that exercise looks like with the thought "I'm terrible at interviews."

- Is it true? Yes, it feels true and I received some negative feedback from my last interview.
- Is it 100% true in all situations or can you think of a time when it wasn't true? Well, I've managed to get jobs so I guess it can't be totally true. And actually I

did receive some positive feedback from that interview I did last month.

- How do you feel when you think that thought? That I'll never get a new job and I'll be stuck in my current job forever, which is depressing.

- How does it make you act? I've stopped applying for jobs as it feels pointless when I'm going to mess up the interview. No point in putting myself through that.

- Who would you be without that thought? Someone who confidently applied for jobs and believed she could get the job.

- How do you want to feel? Confident, not dreading interviews or feeling like a failure.

- What would you need to believe to feel the way you want to feel? That I can improve my interviewing skills, that interviews are just an opportunity to get to know each other better and that when I am the right person for the job they will know.

- What belief would you like to have going forward? I'm improving my interviewing skills and interviews are just a way of meeting people and seeing if the fit is there for both parties.

When you are creating your new belief, you want it to feel possible or your brain will reject it. If you said *"I am amazing at interviews,"* that would not ring true so choose a belief that is both helpful and realistic such as *"I am improving my interview skills and building my confidence."*

4. Embed your new belief

It takes repetition and action to embed a new belief. You could:

- Use it as a silent affirmation while you brush your teeth for two minutes in the morning.
- Write it on a sticky note by your laptop if you work from home.
- Write it out ten times a day.
- Ask yourself – if I truly believed this, what action would I take today? Then take that action. For example, you could read an article about interview techniques.

As with the Inner Critic, working on your unhelpful beliefs is an ongoing process. You will keep on uncovering new ones, but you'll get better at spotting them rather than taking them at face value. One of the benefits of working with a coach is that often they can spot an unhelpful belief that you still think is a fact. You don't need to reframe all your beliefs overnight (in fact, please don't) – pick one that is holding you back currently and start there.

Worrying less about work

Another unhelpful coping strategy many of us have adopted is worrying.

I had a lifelong worry habit. I experienced anxiety as a child – I worried a lot about what people thought of me and was terrified of making mistakes. That didn't magically disappear when I became an adult. When I became a manager, then a head of team and even as a director and CEO I still worried about so many things. I worried about what my team thought of me and if I was good enough at managing and leading. I worried about not hitting targets and the consequences of that. I'd have a conversation and then worry that I'd said the wrong thing.

I worried because worrying gave me the illusion of control. My logic was that if I could just think through all the scenarios then I'd be better able to cope with them if they happened. Even though worrying didn't make me feel good, I thought it was helping me to reduce the uncertainty that I didn't want to deal with.

The reason we worry is because at some level we think it works. We think it's helpful for us. If you too are a worrier then at some point in your life your brain decided worry was a useful coping strategy, and now it has become a habit. That habit is probably making you unhappy, because when we are busy worrying about what can go wrong, we are rarely focused on what is going right.

When we worry we also flood our brain with negative thoughts, which makes us see the world in a more negative light. Our brain has so much information coming at it throughout the day that to avoid overwhelm it seeks out information which confirms what it already knows (and disregards information that contradicts what it already knows). This is known as confirmation bias. So when our thoughts focus on what can go wrong, we are training our brain to seek out information that confirms those worries and ignore the information that contradicts them. It makes us overestimate risk and see connections between events that are not actually there.

For example, you might be worried about raising an issue with your line manager which you think will cause tension. Perhaps you've even run scenarios in your head that end with you leaving the organization as the tension becomes unbearable. You have the conversation. It goes okay. But then the next day your line manager is short with you on a call. Your mind immediately jumps to the conclusion that your career is indeed doomed and you should never have had that conversation. They could just be having a bad day, but your brain has taken that as evidence to confirm what it had already decided was the truth.

I run a masterclass on worry and at the start I ask the women attending what they worry about and what impact worrying has on them. I want to share their answers with you because it will help you to feel less alone in your worry.

"I worry about messing up and that something bad will happen because I've missed something."

"I worry that I'm focusing on the wrong things."

"I worry that I won't be able to deliver on what I've promised."

"I worry that I won't be able to get everything done and I'll let people down."

"I worry that I've said the wrong thing and upset someone without even realizing it."

"I worry about what other people think of me."

"I repeat negative feedback in my head over and over again."

"I worry about my team and not being able to protect them."

"I worry about how I'm going to get my work done and still be on time for nursey and school pick-ups."
"I worry that I'm not good enough."

These worries were impacting their sleep. Some couldn't fall asleep as their head was whirring replaying the day. Others woke up at 2am thinking about work and couldn't get back to sleep.

This was impacting their sense of wellbeing as their heads were full of work and worry, meaning they felt stressed and lost perspective. Some were doubting themselves to the point of looking for a new, less senior role.

These worries were affecting their work as they procrastinated and delayed making decisions because they were worried about making the wrong decision.

And these worries were impacting their relationships as they struggled to be in the moment with their kids or would take their stress out on friends and family.

Worry is particularly prevalent among high-achieving women who appear calm and confident on the outside. We are high functioning externally, yet our internal talk is often dominated by worry and self-doubt.

Five mental strategies to reduce worry

You can use mental strategies to help you worry less and I'm going to share five of these here.

1. Manage your mental energy

Think about your mental energy as a battery. It's a rechargeable battery that you can charge with sleep, doing things you enjoy, self-care and spending time with loved ones. But you've got to get through the day on that charge and as you use up your mental and emotional energy your battery level goes down. If you've ever come home from work too exhausted to do anything but collapse on the couch then you'll know the feeling when your battery has run out.

Your mental and emotional energy is your most precious resource when it comes to work. It's your personality. Your get up and go. It's what encourages your colleagues to listen to you, what inspires them. It's what helps you do your job well and what gets you up in the morning feeling positive about the day.

As you go through your day you expend your energy. You expend it reading emails, sitting in meetings or on video calls, on decision making, dealing with problems and of course on worrying.

Where are you expending your mental energy? And what percentage of it are you expending on worrying?

> *"When you asked me how much energy I expended on worry yesterday I realized it was about 50%!" Hannah*

If you are expending any of your precious energy on worry then it isn't available for you to use for the things that matter. There is a significant cost to worrying. And I want you to understand that because it is a crucial part of building the case in your mind against worrying as your chosen coping strategy. We want to help your brain realize that worry is not helping you after all.

When you catch yourself worrying, I'd like you to think:

"Is this where I want to focus my mental energy?"

Wouldn't it be great to have some of that mental energy left for yourself and your loved ones at the end of the day? From now on you can consciously *choose* if you want to invest that energy in worrying.

2. Shift your attention

There are two types of worries: productive and unproductive.

You know a worry is productive if it is realistic or plausible *and* if you can do something about it right now or very soon. If your worry meets those criteria, I encourage you to move into action quickly.

Worried about taking the *wrong* action? Often we get scared of taking the wrong action, particularly if we tend toward perfectionism. That's because we believe in the myth that there is only one right answer. In fact, in most situations there are a number of potential actions you can take to get you the result you want. You are better off taking some action which will move you forward and give you information than you are staying paralyzed by fear. You can always course correct if you need to, but if you stay stuck then you have no new information, and your head keeps going round in circles.

All worries that don't meet the criteria above are unproductive. If you have an unproductive worry you can shift your attention with this simple question:

"Where can I most productively focus my attention right now?"

Being a better leader, and a happier person, involves asking yourself better questions to improve the quality of your thoughts. If we ask ourselves a question, then our brains naturally want to close the loop by answering it.

And if you're overwhelmed and your mind comes up blank in answer to the question above, then focus on gratitude and make a list of the things you are grateful for in that moment. It will shift your mood as well as your attention.

3. Turn your overthinking into a superpower

If you have a naturally busy brain, you can use that power for good and focus it on analysis rather than worry. When you find yourself worrying, grab a pen and paper and use one of these two tools to get the thoughts out of your brain and onto paper.

Conduct an audit

If your worries focus on the past and you often replay events in your head wondering if you could have handled them better, then this is the tool for you. You can ask yourself these questions…

"What went well?"
"What didn't go so well?"
"What will I do differently next time?"

This gives you a balanced view rather than focusing on the negatives. It also helps you to develop a growth mindset as you see everything as a learning opportunity rather than as either successful or a failure.

Scenario planning

If your worries focus on the future, you can scenario plan by mapping out the different possible options or outcomes and what you would do in each of those scenarios.

Your brain thinks it is already doing this by worrying, but actually it's going round and round on a hamster wheel, without any sense of completion. Writing the options down gives you that sense of completion and the ability to look at the situation logically.

4. Ditch the to-do list

I love a list. But having an epically long to-do list just keeps you focused on all the things that still need to be done. To-do lists are never ending as there will always be more you can do. So put your to-do list in a drawer, somewhere you can't see it, and replace it with a *top three things to do today list*. It will help you stay really focused. Pick the three tasks that will make the biggest impact. When you complete those three tasks you'll feel a sense of satisfaction and success.

You can also add a *done list* where you track what you've done each day and give yourself a high five for what you've achieved.

5. Be in the moment

When we worry, our minds are rarely in the present moment. They're busy replaying the past or predicting the future. We can't change the past. And try as we might, we can't control the future. We are literally wasting our precious energy and hours of our lives worrying.

We can't cope with something hasn't happened yet. We can only respond to what is happening now, in this moment. And in this moment, even if things are far from ideal, you are coping. *Everything is okay in this moment.* This is a mantra I use when something scary is happening and I feel fear sending me into a downward spiral.

We can train ourselves to get better at living in the moment by meditating, doing yoga or simply going for a walk and noticing what is around us. I'm a big fan of the Japanese concept of *shinrin yoku* or forest bathing and head to my local wood when I feel overwhelmed to soak up the calm energy of trees (I've been known to hug one). You can also ground yourself by noticing the sensation of your feet on the floor for 10 seconds.

How do I recover from a bullying boss?
See page 191.

Chapter 2: Top tips

- Your value as a person is not connected to the quality of your work.

- You can strategically choose how much effort to put into tasks to manage your time and energy effectively.

- Done is better than perfect and good is good enough most of the time.

- When you are worrying ask yourself, *"Where can I most productively focus my attention right now?"*

- Turn your overthinking into a strength by conducting an audit or scenario planning instead of worrying.

- Swap your epic to-do list for a three things list or a done list.

Chapter 3

Dealing with the tough days

Leadership is a privilege but it can also be exhausting and demotivating at times and it's important to build our resilience so that we can handle the tough days. In this chapter we'll be looking at how to avoid burnout, how to stay motivated when you're exhausted and how to deal with feedback gracefully. Plus I'll be sharing my top tips on how to say no without creating conflict.

Avoiding burnout

A recent survey of 7,500 employees by Gallup found that 23% of them reported often feeling burnt out, and 44% reported sometimes feeling burnt out.[1] I come across a lot of burnout when coaching but interestingly people often don't recognize what they are experiencing as burnout.

Medically speaking, there are 12 stages of burnout.[2] I've noticed five stages my clients experience, but they are not always linear as people can bounce around them depending on what's going on for them at work and personally.

1. Pre-burnout – the adrenaline rush

You're working crazy-hard but you are feeling good. You're focused, performing well and are prepared to put in the extra hours to succeed. Usually this happens in a new role or when working on a new project but it can also happen during a crisis and we saw a lot of this in the initial COVID-19 lockdown.

2. The energy dip

It's hard to sustain that level of energy long term but you now expect yourself to keep delivering at that level. Anything else feels like failure. You're working long hours, sacrificing personal boundaries and priorities for work and feeling tired.

3. Constantly stressed and frustrated

You're running on low energy and find yourself feeling frequently frustrated with others, particularly those who don't seem as committed as you. This can also show up physically with aches and pain or getting lots of bugs.

4. Motivation vortex

Usually highly motivated, you have zero desire to work. Monday mornings make you groan. Things that would have got you riled up now make you shrug your shoulders in defeat. You simply don't have the physical, mental or emotional energy to fully engage in work and you feel very guilty about that because it is so unlike you. People often start thinking that they need a new career path at this point.

5. Hit the wall

You've hit the wall and literally can't function. You are exhausted – this looks different for different people. At this point people leave jobs or get signed off sick because continuing is not an option.

In my own burnout story I experienced all of these. I was in a director of fundraising and marketing role in a charity and I'd come into a situation that needed turning around quickly. Doing that involved expending a huge amount of energy to turn a disconnected and unhappy team into a happy and high-performing team. I really wanted to prove to myself and everyone else that I deserved this role and there was a lot of responsibility on my shoulders, since without doubling our annual income that year we'd be making cuts to vital charitable services as well as making redundancies.

We turned it around, built a wonderful team and doubled our annual income. But I struggled to enjoy that success at the time. I was emotionally over-invested and really gave it my all so when decisions were made that made it harder to do my job or piled on more expectations, I became increasingly frustrated. I would fight every battle because they all felt important, and I can see now that I needed to be right all of the time. I eventually reached a point where I no longer wanted any responsibility. Just as things had really turned around and I'd done all the hard work laying the foundations for success, I quit.

I learned some lessons about how to avoid burnout going forward that I share with my coaching clients.

1. Know your burnout warning signs

Notice how you feel, think and act when you are running low on energy so that when you see those signs you can recognize it as overworking or heading toward burnout. For me it begins with the inability to switch off and an overwhelming need to tick things off the to-do list. Then I start making mistakes and getting clumsy. At the end of my working day, I want to sleep rather than talk to friends and eventually I lose my motivation and mojo altogether and have to take a week off work to reset.

2. Check you are in a healthy work situation

Sometimes we burn out because too much is being asked of us, we are trying to survive in a toxic environment, or we are simply in the wrong job and performing poorly as a result. If your friends and family are telling you to leave your job it is probably time to take their advice seriously. We often stay in situations when we would advise a friend in the same situation to leave straight away. It takes courage to leave but sometimes you reach a point where your mental health requires it. Ali, a client of mine, had the dream job on paper but in reality she was fighting a constant stream of negativity and it was burning her out. After much deliberating she chose to walk away and take a break from work.

> *"I've had such a lovely summer with the kids and it was a huge relief to walk away from all the internal politics. I'm delighted to share that next month I start my dream job and I can already tell it's a much better working environment. I just wish I'd not stayed so long when I knew it was bad for me."* Ali

3. Build rest into your week

Avoid overscheduling and having endless back-to-back meetings. Create moments of space in your daily and weekly diary. Moments to think, take a walk or actually enjoy that cup of tea. Those moments will give you the breathing space you need to keep going. Even just ending some meetings ten minutes earlier will help. If you are highly driven, remind yourself that this is a marathon not a sprint and it serves no-one if you work yourself into the ground.

4. Know yourself

Get to know your work patterns – what causes you stress and how much stress is healthy for you. I learned that I love to work in change situations, but I needed to avoid over-investing and so interim roles turned out to be the perfect fit for me. I could add huge value and do what I enjoyed without sacrificing myself in the process.

5. Focus on what is within your control

Stephen Covey talks about the circle of control (things within your control), the circle of influence (things you may be able to influence) and the circle of concern (things which impact you but you can't control or influence).[3] Don't waste your energy on the things in that final circle.

6. Use your energy wisely

According to the Pareto principle, 20% of our work leads to 80% of our results. You could try and identify the 20% of your work that leads to 80% of your results. Then if you focus on that and drop the less impactful busy work you will become more productive and work less.

Being kind to yourself

If we want to avoid burnout we need to start being kinder to ourselves. Society tells us that women are expected to be kind and nurturing and look after everyone's needs except our own. In a fantastic interview with Oprah, Shonda Rhimes, creator of *Grey's Anatomy* and *Scandal*, rightly pointed out that many Mother's Day cards celebrated the sacrifices that mothers had made for their children and we were teaching girls to celebrate being selfless and put aside their needs in a way we don't with boys.[4]

We can keep playing out that same old narrative or we can break the cycle for future generations, starting with how we treat ourselves. We need to take responsibility for our own happiness, which includes knowing what our needs are, asking for what we need and not putting so much pressure on ourselves.

No-one wants to become a selfish person but *you are allowed to be selfish sometimes.* Everyone else is and perhaps the reason we sometimes feel resentful of that is because we don't give ourselves that gift. Give yourself permission to make a choice that works for you even though it may not be optimal for others. *Give yourself permission to focus on what you want to do instead of what you should do.*

Lola, one of the women in my Influence & Impact course, worried that if she started taking care of herself by not working so hard then she might go too far and be lazy. I asked her *"Why aren't you allowed to be lazy sometimes? Why aren't you allowed to just rest and do nothing?"* If we look at kids running around full of energy, they need to go and lie down on the sofa for a while or have a nap and restore their energy before they can get up and run around again. We do all the work (and often more than our fair share of the home running, life admin and child rearing) without ever giving ourselves the rest to restore our energy.

In my experience, the pressure to do it all and go above and beyond isn't external. Our expectations of ourselves are often higher than the expectations that others place on us. And then we feel like we are failing when we don't meet them.

Here are three simple questions that you can ask yourself regularly to help you be kinder to yourself:

"What would I say to a friend in this situation?"
"If I was being kind to myself, what would I do right now?"
"What do I need in this moment?"

Invest some time in self-care too. Self-care is more than a bubble bath or a massage. In fact, science tells us we need to be kind to ourselves. Dr Paul Gilbert, author of *The Compassionate Mind*, shares a fascinating model about how we regulate our emotions. We have three emotional regulation systems:[5]

- The Threat system – this is about managing threats and keeping you safe. When activated, it floods your body with adrenaline and cortisol.
- The Drive system – this is about achievement and progress. Every time we tick something off the to-do list, we get a dopamine hit.
- The Soothing system – this is about managing stress and promoting bonding and it creates oxytocin (the hug hormone).

When I share this model with my coaching clients, they usually recognize that they spend their time bouncing between the Threat and Drive system. Toward the end of their time in Influence & Impact, they spend less time in the Threat system and are mainly in the Drive system with the occasional dip into the Soothing system. I would stay in the Drive system all day everyday if I could and have had to learn to look after myself. We all need more time in the Soothing system than we actually give ourselves but it is essential for our health as well as our performance at work.

The other challenge with being kinder to yourself is that it often involves saying no to other people. It can feel uncomfortable as we are so used to saying yes to everything, but when you say no to something you don't want to do, it feels empowering. Could you start saying no to social engagements when you're exhausted or stop being the person who takes on the tasks no-one else volunteers for in meetings? What are you currently saying yes to that you would like to say no to?

If saying no is hard, start with "not this time" or "not now." You can say sorry if that makes it feel easier. But try working your way up to saying no without over-apologizing for having your own needs and priorities, as an individual and as a leader. No is a complete sentence but I rarely respond with a flat no. I'm more likely to say "Now isn't a good time" or "The team doesn't have the capacity for that at the moment" or "That isn't aligned with our priorities for this quarter."

Handling negative feedback well

Even the most confident of female leaders can struggle to deal with negative feedback or criticism. When you're working hard and doing your best, such feedback can be demotivating or even really knock your confidence. The feedback, and then the stories that you tell yourself about that feedback, can dominate your thoughts for hours, if not days. So let's see if we can make it easier to handle.

Why we find negative feedback so hard

We need to feel that we are making progress at work to feel satisfied. This is known as the Progress Principle.[6] If we experience a setback, or perceived setback, in that progress it can hit us hard. In fact, the negative impact of feeling like we've taken a step backwards is almost three times as powerful as the equivalent boost from making progress.

When somebody criticizes or gives us negative feedback about an element of our work or a specific piece of work that we've done, we often make it mean something. We make it mean that they don't value us. We make it mean that they haven't seen the hard work that we put in. We make it mean that we don't have a future in this organization, or that we're being treated unfairly.

And perhaps some of those things are true, but often, we are making extra meaning that simply isn't there. It doesn't mean anything about you as a person. *It simply means that that piece of work needed more improvement.*

We can't get rid of negative feedback altogether. It is simply impossible to be perfect. And as I covered in

Chapter 2 on mastering your mindset, I'm not even sure it's something that we should be aspiring to. We are going to do things imperfectly and we are going to get feedback on that. So we need to get better at dealing with that reality, and not take that feedback and make it into something that makes us unhappy.

How do we deal with negative feedback professionally and positively?

Adopt a growth mindset

We can work on increasing our resilience and adopting what Dr Carol Dweck calls a "growth mindset."[7] Dweck says there are two types of mindset: fixed and growth. With a fixed mindset you believe that your abilities are fixed. If you fail, it means something about you, so you avoid failure at all costs. Negative feedback hits you hard if you've got a fixed mindset.

With a growth mindset you believe that you have infinite potential to learn and grow and improve. You see failure as the useful provision of information to help you move forward. You can potentially get better at everything so negative feedback allows you to refine your skills.

I've worked hard to develop my growth mindset. In my first few jobs I was devastated by negative feedback, but in time I came to see how valuable constructive criticism could be.

As a new managing director of a recruitment company, I hadn't realized how quickly a cashflow crisis could occur until we had one. I found myself frantically calling clients to get our bills paid. I thought I was dealing with that well because I went into problem-solving mode. I was on call after call collecting in the money that we were owed. But the owner of the company took me aside and said, "You are panicking everybody, because your face is showing that you are clearly stressed out and your panic will be contagious. People will start to worry unnecessarily because of how you're dealing with this."

I'll be honest; I had a moment of wanting to cry. But I very quickly realized that that was valuable feedback. I had no idea I was making a negative impact. And thanks to that feedback I was able to have an honest conversation with my team about what was going on and let them know that everything was going to be fine. And it was growth mindset that allowed me to do that rather than emotionally spiraling and quitting.

Avoid emotionally overinvesting in work

You can care about your work without being emotionally overinvested in it. As we've discussed, when your self-esteem and sense of identity is too closely tied to your job it can make you super-sensitive to feedback. Notice if you're getting your sense of value, your sense of meaning and worth entirely from work (and I have been in that place in the past) and then try and rebalance; try to remember who you are outside of work, try to remember that you are more than a job title and your achievements and to-do list.

Stick to the facts

There are two separate things going on with that negative feedback:

1. There is what they said (the fact), e.g., *"This wasn't up to standard."*
2. There is what you make it mean (the story), e.g., *"I'm terrible at my job."*

We want to listen to the facts and try not to leap straight to the story. When you go back and play the conversation back in your head afterwards, try and focus instead on the actual words they used without adding meaning. Then see if you can come up with a new story that doesn't make you feel terrible. You can write this down to help you process it.

Responding professionally

Try and remember that there have been times as a leader that you have had to deliver negative feedback, or what might have felt like criticism to people that work for you. But your intention was to make them better at their job. It may help to assume the person giving you feedback has those same good intentions.

Keep it simple and say *"Thank you for the feedback."* Don't jump to defending yourself, just say thank you and then you can go away and think about it.

Another phrase you can use is *"I'd like to go and reflect on that. Can I come back to you with some questions later if I have any?"*

Or *"I'm sorry to hear that; I hadn't realized this was an issue. Please can you tell me more about what you feel should have been done differently?"*

If you're not clear, ask questions to get clarity on what specifically better looks like, because often we come away knowing we did something wrong but unsure of how to improve going forward.

A quick note on assuming good intentions. If the person giving you feedback has shown themselves to be a fair person, it can help to focus on the positives. However, "good intentions" is never an excuse for discriminatory feedback and sadly that phrase has been used to dismiss too many valid claims of discrimination in the workplace, in particular racism. Please know that I am not encouraging you to dismiss or accept discrimination. Good intentions do not justify unacceptable behavior.

If you disagree with the feedback

If, on reflection, you disagree with the feedback then you may want to respond differently. Unless the situation calls for it you want to avoid being aggressive or defensive. Unfortunately, women are judged for showing any significant emotion in the workplace and while men can show anger without consequences, we cannot. I hope that changes as we see more women lead and as we call it out. Women of color and black women are often subject to unfair labeling as aggressive and as women we can support each other to call out discriminatory labeling and behavior when we see it.

If you want to challenge feedback (of a non-discriminatory nature) you might want to say: *"Thank you for your feedback. That is one perspective on what happened, an alternative perspective is…"* or *"I appreciate the feedback and having reflected on it I'd like to offer an alternative perspective."*

If you feel that they want you to do something their way but your way is equally valid you can say: *"I know that approach works really well for you; I believe my approach is an alternative way to achieve the result we are both committed to, can I talk you through my reasoning?"*

Taking it on board

Do you respect the person who is giving you feedback? Do they know what they're talking about on this subject? If the answer to one or both of these questions is yes, I suggest you do think about taking it on board.

You can start seeing feedback as information that you can use to course correct rather than something bad that happens to you. Look for the silver lining. Is this person pointing out a blind spot that you were unaware of, much like the feedback I received about causing panic? Have they identified some skills you need to develop to be even better at your job or rise to the next level? Both of those insights will help you to develop yourself as a leader.

How do I keep myself motivated in challenging times? See page 195.

Chapter 3: Top tips

- Get to know your burnout warning signs.

- Focus on the things within your circle of control.

- Notice whether you are in Fear, Drive or Soothing mode and spend more time in Soothing mode.

- Ask yourself *"What do I need in this moment?"*

- Start saying no more often.

- Adopt a growth mindset to help you appreciate feedback more.

Part 2

Being seen as a leader by others

Now that you are starting to see yourself as the leader that you are, it's time to think about how you're coming across to other people and learn how to step into your authority so that you are seen as a leader by others too.

In this section we're going to look at some of the key "touchpoints" in the working day that give you the opportunity to demonstrate your leadership. We're also going to look at some of the practical tools and techniques that will help, as well as some of the common mistakes to avoid!

Chapter 4 – Leading with confidence

By being intentional about how you are perceived by others and avoiding the mistakes that many managers unknowingly make, you'll be able to step into a more confident leadership style.

Chapter 5 – Communicating with clarity

If you've sat in meetings where you've been interrupted, had your contribution "hepeated" or been put on the spot, then this chapter's Meeting Toolkit and tips on speaking up will be invaluable.

Chapter 4

Leading with confidence

Leading with confidence is about leading your way rather than trying to be like the leaders you may be comparing yourself to. In this chapter you'll be uncovering your Personal Leadership Brand – your own authentic and powerful style of leading. Then we'll explore the management mistakes that make it harder to do your job and how you can overcome those, step into your authority and build your credibility as a manager. Finally, we'll cover how to delegate effectively so that the only things are on your plate are the things that should be on it.

Developing your Personal Leadership Brand

Great leaders are clear about the impact and impression that they want to make on others. I call this your Personal Leadership Brand. Getting this right can open up career opportunities, improve your performance and help you stand out within your organization. So let's get intentional about how you want to be perceived by others.

You already have a Personal Leadership Brand – you just haven't taken control of it yet! It's what others say about you when you aren't in the room. It's what your team thinks of your management style. It's how your line manager feels about you and how colleagues describe you. It's about how much potential your CEO sees in you and whether you are seen as a leader.

But this isn't about being a perfect cookie-cutter version of a leader or trying to be like someone else. *I want you to be more you at work, not less you.* This process is about empowering you to lead *your* way.

Many of us are stuck in a comparison trap. We look at other leaders and compare ourselves unfavorably to them. We then proceed to "should" all over ourselves – we "should" be more analytical, more inspiring, more confident, more extroverted, more reflective. Of course, unbeknown to us everyone else is comparing themselves unfavorably to others too. Instead of comparing ourselves to others we want to feel good about the way we lead.

Organizations need diversity to thrive and as leaders we need to be authentic to build connection and respect. When someone is not being authentic we can tell at some unconscious level and we distrust them. An authentic leader, on the other hand, communicates in a way that resonates with others and implicitly gives them permission to embrace who they are as well. That is a huge gift to give someone.

It's time to reflect upon about what kind of leader you want to be, your unique combination of skills, experience and personality and what your organization needs from you. From there you can create your own Personal Leadership Brand and use it as a tool to build your career.

For this coaching exercise you'll need a paper and pen. Jot down your answers to the questions below on one piece of paper so that by the end of the exercise you have a paper filled with words and phrases.

Step 1 – What kind of leader do you want to be?

Think of two leaders that you admire and write down what it was that you admire about their leadership style. Is it how they communicate? How they make others feel? The action they take?

Hopefully that has given you some inspiration so that you can now think about what kind of leader *you* would like to be. Often we fall into managing and leading and don't create time to reflect on this. How would you like others to describe your leadership style? How do you want to make them feel? Note down all your answers.

Step 2 – What do you uniquely bring to leadership?

Next we are going to uncover your superpowers. These are the things that come very naturally to you, you are brilliant at and that energize you.

Your Inner Critic may already be telling you that you don't have any superpowers! Rest assured that you do, because we all do. *You don't have the be the world's best at something for it to be your superpower.* I have a friend who has the superpower of making whoever she is talking to feel special by giving them her full attention. I've seen superpowers ranging from problem-solving to inspiring others and being uber-organized. My own superpowers include radical honesty and bringing together groups of amazing women by creating a safe space for them.

So have fun with this. Think of all the things you love to do. Think of what people say when they give you nice feedback. Think about how others see you. Ask your best friend at work what they think your superpowers are. Consider what exactly it is that makes you great at your job. Don't compare yourself to anyone else; instead tune in to your Inner Leader. Add your superpowers to the list on your piece of paper.

One final note on superpowers. When I do this exercise in a live workshop, I ask the women attending to share their superpower and really own it by stating *"My superpower is"* or *"I am brilliant at…"* Many find this incredibly hard and yet I am sure that a room full of men would have no problems doing that!

As women we are unaccustomed to shouting about our successes or pointing out our strengths. And we get embarrassed when someone else does it for us. We need to get more comfortable with owning our awesomeness. Every time we do that, we show other women and girls that it is safe to shine.

Start by accepting compliments with a simple *"thank you"* instead of shrugging them off. Then try putting yourself forward for a task involving your superpower by saying *"I'm good at X so I can help with that"* or *"That is one of my strengths so I'm happy to lead on that."*

Will it feel uncomfortable at first? Probably. Is it boasting? No. It's stating a fact and sharing where your skills can add value. If we want the next generation of women to be as powerful and influential as their male counterparts we can help by modeling how to own our superpowers, so if it feels awkward doing so for yourself, try doing it for the next generation.

Step 3 – What does your organization need from you?

As leaders we don't operate in a vacuum and our Personal Leadership Brand needs to work within the context of our organization and at this point in time. I often see leaders who were successful in their previous company flounder in a new company because they've not adapted their approach to the new environment. Equally, if your organization is in a period of intense change or in crisis, your approach to leading will need to change accordingly.

Identify your top priorities as a leader for the next 6–12 months. Then think about what sort of leadership attributes you need to achieve each of those priorities. For example, if you are leading on a large project you might need to be consultative, structured and inspiring. Write down those attributes. Not all of those attributes will be things you excel at and that's okay.

If you lead a team or project, then write down what kind of leadership you think your team members need from you over the next 6–12 months too.

Finally, given this exercise is about developing your career, think about what leadership attributes are valued within your organization. What do people get celebrated for? Do people get celebrated for collaborating or competing, for example? Look at what leadership styles the people at the top of your organization or those who get promoted have in common. Consider the way your leaders communicate and what it says about what they value. Write down any words that sum up what your organization values.

Step 4 – Create your power words

Now we want to refine that page of words and phrases down into three words or phrases.

Start by reviewing the page and highlighting or circling around ten words or phrases that really resonate with you or jump out at you. Pick the words that you'd like others to use to describe you when you are not in the room. Some of those words might describe you as you are now, others might be more aspirational and that's fine.

Once you have those ten words, transfer them to a new sheet of paper and look for any crossover between words or any words that could be combined into a more powerful word or phrase. For example, I'm a change maker and I love to leave places better than I find them so for me "a positive force for good" was a phrase that summed up both of those points.

Keep on playing with the words until you narrow it down to just three words or phrases. Your power words are your Personal Leadership Brand. Don't worry – you don't need a well-crafted statement as this isn't something you'll be sharing with others. You just need simple words and phrases that you can easily remember.

Step 5 – Use your Personal Leadership Brand

You can remind yourself of your power words before you go into meetings, or before sending a tricky email. They will act as a subconscious filter which will support you in showing up as the kind of leader you want to be. For example, if one of your words is strategic then when you have moments of wanting to dive into the detail, you'll remember that the strategic thing to do is to look at the bigger picture.

You can also dial up your power words. How much are you really embodying your power words currently? Rate yourself out of 10 for each one and then pick the lowest one and ask yourself what you could do this week to increase that by one point. For example, if you have rated yourself 7 out of 10 for being collaborative, what could you do this week to get closer to an 8 out of 10 rating?

"When I did the Personal Leadership Brand exercise I wanted to be seen as inspiring, supportive and expert. I focused on showing up like that every day and three weeks later one of the senior leaders in the company mentioned me as an example of an inspiring leader!" Gita

Being intentional about your behavior is powerful. As is connecting to what is important to you as a leader and what you uniquely bring. This exercise has empowered hundreds of women to own their leadership style and do it their way instead of comparing themselves to others.

Top tip

You can also use a micro version of this method for an interview or a particular meeting. Simply think beforehand about how you would like people to describe you after the meeting and it will help you to go in feeling focused. If you have a colleague that you'd like to listen to you, you might want to be seen as an expert, for example. Or if you are interviewing for a job at the next level up it would be great to be seen as credible.

Leading your team

Now you've established what your Personal Leadership Brand is, the next step to being seen as a leader is to stop making the following five common management mistakes.

Mistake 1 – Claiming all the RESPONSIBILITY that comes with your job title and none of the AUTHORITY

You know you're doing this if:

- you don't set clear expectations and boundaries as you don't want to be seen as demanding;
- the tasks you delegate boomerang back to you, or people don't carry out the tasks you allocate to them;
- team members miss deadlines or ignore the emails they don't want to answer;
- you are super grateful, acting like people have done you a huge favor when they are just doing their jobs.

Many of us feel more comfortable with responsibility than authority. From a young age females are encouraged to embrace responsibility and be responsible. No-one teaches us how to have authority. We might feel that we don't have natural authority. We probably don't want to be like the managers that we disliked who misused their authority. We don't want to be judged or considered demanding. Plus there's a narrative that powerful women are not likable.

But if you're not claiming the authority that comes with your job title then you aren't operating like a leader at your level. So here is my favorite coaching tool to help you do that.

Coaching tool: The Cloak of Authority

I was 29 when I took on my first director role and as part of the interview process I met members of my team. After I'd been hired, I discovered that those team members had thought I was too young for the role and had not supported my appointment. I clearly didn't have a lot of natural authority!

The team was struggling after a difficult period and some of them were openly challenging my authority to lead and make changes. I was having challenging conversations that Carla the person did not want to have (I hate conflict and want to be liked as much as anyone else) but Carla the director needed to have.

I was also having to deliver bad news about income to a board of trustees, prove to people that I deserved this director role and hold my own in conversations with CEOs and celebrities. I needed to have more authority to be able to do my job well.

It took me a while to realize that my authority didn't need to come from me, because my job title came with authority. And so does yours!

At the time, the Harry Potter films were hitting the cinemas. In the first film Harry is given an invisibility cloak for Christmas and when he wears it he becomes invisible. So I decided to create some magical clothing of my own... *The Cloak of Authority.*

Whenever I had to go into a challenging meeting I would imagine myself putting on my Cloak of Authority and claiming the authority that came with my job title. Studies tell us that tools like this, alongside affirmations and power posing, add to our sense of self-efficacy and allow us to feel more in control.[1] Putting on my Cloak of Authority made me feel empowered and helped me to stick to what I planned to say instead of wimping out for fear of judgment. My body language was different, my voice was lower, my speech was slower and I was able to sit with any uncomfortable silence.

> *"Thank you so much for the Cloak of Authority tool. I put it on for a meeting with my fellow directors this week and for once I didn't let them dismiss my input."* Caroline

Hundreds of women have used this simple technique to have challenging conversations. It is a tool you can now call on whenever you need to feel like you have more authority.

Simply imagine putting on your Cloak of Authority and claiming the authority that comes with your job title.

Setting expectations

One of the ways we fail to claim the authority that goes with our job title is when we avoid setting expectations. We worry about being judged for setting expectations but in fact, when it comes to expectations, people value clarity. It helps no-one if a team member is not delivering because they don't know what good delivery is meant to look like. And you do have expectations – you just aren't sharing them and are probably getting frustrated when they are not being met! So do make sure that you are clearly articulating what good performance looks like, as well as any deadlines and the reasons for those deadlines and standards of performance.

The next step is holding people accountable to their commitments. When someone fails to deliver upon a commitment, you don't want them to feel like it's no big deal. You want them to know that that is going to cause you issues and that they are not meeting your expectations. To be clear, it's not about shaming them – it's about helping them to be good at their jobs and build trust.

If someone fails to deliver, rather than say *"That's okay"* (when it really isn't okay), try leaving a bit of silence and putting them on the spot. You could use a phrase like *"Oh, I thought we were clear on the deadline… why hasn't it been done?"*. Tone is crucial here – you want to sound firm but fair, not harsh.

Their response will probably be about being too busy. You can then be clear that next time you expect them to let you know ahead of time if something can't be done and you need to be able to trust that when you pass something to them, they will deliver. You can also talk to them about prioritizing as carrying out a task you've allocated to them should be a priority and they may have too much on their plate.

If you'd like to stop being super grateful, keep saying *"please"* and *"thank you"* but leave off the superlatives – no need to say *"Thank you soooo much I really appreciate it"* unless someone is going above and beyond their job. Everyone deserves good manners, but praise needs to be linked to effort or performance to actually mean anything.

Mistake 2 – Avoiding difficult conversations because you want to be liked

We all want to be liked – it's a human need. But it is impossible to be liked by everyone all the time, especially when you are managing and leading. During your career it is extremely likely that you'll have to make tough decisions, mediate between team members, communicate bad news and disappoint people. You'll also need to tackle tensions between your team and other teams, push back when arguing crucial points with peers and deliver feedback which may not be welcomed.

In those moments people may not like what you have to say, but you *can* still be a likable person. How likable you are is about how you treat people and how you show up daily; it's not about never having difficult conversations. People will respect you for being honest and for tackling problems.

It is kinder to let someone know that there is an issue than to ignore it and hope it will go away. Most problems within organizations are better tackled than swept under the carpet. Being the person who will tackle issues boldly and with kindness and empathy will help you to be seen as a leader.

If you need a bit of courage to have the hard conversations you can use your Cloak of Authority.

Mistake 3 – Fluffing the feedback

Linked to the mistake above, managers often hold back on giving feedback because it feels uncomfortable. Feedback is how people improve but while it can be simple to give feedback on a piece of work, it often feels tougher to give feedback on behavior. You might find yourself watering it down to the point where they have no idea what you are really saying. Or showering them with too much praise to make up for it. Here is a simple tool for giving feedback to a team member who needs it…

Behavior – this is the behavior which is causing issues
Consequence – this is why it isn't helpful
Action – this is how I would like you to act instead

I like this tool because often people giving feedback forget to cover one of these points and the recipient walks away not sure exactly what they've done wrong (which can make them feel unsafe), doesn't understand why it is an issue (which can make them feel bullied) or isn't clear how they could do it differently (which can make them feel demotivated).

If their attitude and work is otherwise good, you can put the feedback in that context by setting the scene and then highlight good behavior and performance when you see it. You might start by saying *"Generally I'm really pleased with how you're performing (give an example or two) but there is one area that is causing some concern which I'd like to talk through with you."*

If they generally need a bit of a motivation to improve then make sure your feedback doesn't get lost among all the vague praise you don't really mean. You might want to start by saying *"I'd like to talk about areas for improvement in your performance"* so they immediately understand that this is a serious conversation. If they don't understand that then they may not make the changes that could turn around their performance, and they won't thank you for that when you are later performance-managing them.

Mistake 4 – Not setting and holding boundaries

A boundary is a line that you draw between what is and what is not an acceptable way to treat you or interact with you. There is no universal set of boundaries that we all share; instead, we have to set boundaries that allow us to do our jobs well and align with what is important to us. We need to explain these boundaries when appropriate and stick to them.

> For example, Alicia, an HR manager in an FMCG company, loved her job and really liked her senior colleague but found it really impacted her family time when her colleague sent messages and asked her to take work calls at weekends. As a member of Influence & Impact she sought and got

some great advice from other members on how to tackle this. She had a conversation with her colleague, explaining that those messages were disrupting precious family time and that she would respond on her return to work when rested after the weekend. Setting that boundary was a healthy way to address the situation and that boundary was then respected. Had she not addressed it she would have felt upset and frustrated, completely unbeknown to her colleague.

Another Influence & Impact member, Katy, was running a Communications team that supported other departments within an insurance firm. She found it really hard when colleagues arrived at her desk unexpected, told her they needed help and expected her to drop everything and help immediately. Rather than communicate this, Katy would often be brisk in her communication and was sometimes seen as unhelpful as a result. On a coaching call we identified that this way of receiving support requests made her feel ambushed and unvalued. Katy came up with a process she asked people to use and she enforced that – signposting people to the process with a smile and saying tasks would be completed in order of priority. People didn't love it initially as it meant they had to make more effort, but they enjoyed interacting with her more and the work got done.

How do you know if you need to set a boundary? Usually if you are feeling anxiety, anger or resentment about a situation it indicates that there may be a boundary that needs setting. Boundary setting tends to be something we do in response to a situation rather than something we set out when we first interact with someone, but if you have been burnt before by a manager that texts you late at night you might want to set boundaries around out-of-working-hours communication when starting a new job.

We train others how to treat us. If someone consistently steps over your boundaries, but you never tell them you are unhappy with their behavior, then they will assume there is no problem. They won't stop that behavior unless you articulate those boundaries because they can't read your mind.

When you feel like a boundary is being stepped on, first do a quick mental check that it is a reasonable boundary. For example, asking people never to email you in the evenings may not be reasonable as many people work flexible hours but saying that you won't check or respond to emails after working hours is, unless your job requires you to be available.

Once you have decided it is a reasonable boundary then find a fair but firm way of communicating it. The Behavior, Consequence, Action tool comes in useful here too, albeit softened in tone.

Behavior: *"I notice you've been sending me lots of emails late at night."*

Consequence: *"When I see these I find it hard to switch off from work and I need that break to come into work feeling energized in the mornings."*

Action: *"I'm going to turn my work emails off when I leave the office and I'll respond to your emails the next day when I can give them my full attention."*

When I coach the women in my Influence & Impact course on this, they often say they wish they'd learned this before starting their role as now they and their team have fallen into bad habits. It is not too late to press the reset button. You can always say:

"I think we've fallen into some unhelpful habits in our interactions and I'd like to talk about those…"
"I've been thinking about why I come out of our one-to-one meetings feeling frustrated and I've realized it is because…"
"X keeps happening and that doesn't work for me because…"
"Can we press the reset button and start again with…"
"Let's talk about how we work together as a team…"

Does it take courage to have those conversations? Yes! But they are worth it. Some people might bristle initially but when they reflect, they should appreciate the honesty – we are not often given the gift of knowing our impact on others. Some people might dislike your boundaries as it means more work for them but if they are reasonable then that is not your problem. And, as with everything in this book, I am assuming you are dealing with a reasonable person, not a toxic bully.

Do you feel like articulating your boundaries is being demanding? Brené Brown is a leading thinker on both boundaries and leadership. She explains that whether we communicate them or not, we still have boundaries and feeling resentful or angry isn't compassionate. She says: "When we fail to set boundaries and hold people accountable, we feel used and mistreated".[2]

Your needs are important. You don't need to constantly put the needs of others before your own to be a good person. In fact, the only person who is responsible for putting your needs first is you, so if you don't do it then no-one else will!

We have to be able to advocate for own needs if we want to have a healthy relationship with work (or indeed any kind of healthy relationship).

As a manager you might also want to set boundaries or expectations about how you operate as a team. I once joined a team as an interim and on my first day one of my direct reports was very derogatory about members of the Finance team, in front of the rest of her team. I quickly pointed out that while I knew it was frustrating, it wasn't acceptable to speak like that about colleagues and I suggested she directed those comments at the finance system instead. I was clearly signaling a boundary of how we treat others, without shaming her in the process. In that situation it was important to speak publicly and lay down that boundary for the team rather than have a private conversation. She and I built a strong relationship because she respected that boundary from there on in and appreciated my commitment to improving the situation.

As a leader you can also check in with your colleagues to find out if you are overstepping any boundaries. A simple question to ask is *"Am I doing anything that makes you job harder?"* or *"Are you happy with the way I communicate with you? Is there anything you'd like me to do differently?"* Then listen, without being defensive, and respect their boundaries.

Mistake 5 – Taking responsibility for your team's happiness

I have coached a lot of leaders who have huge amounts of empathy and go to bed at night worrying about their team members, particularly during periods of change. Yet that worrying isn't helping anyone.

Another member of Influence & Impact, Carolina, had to put her entire team on furlough during the first COVID-19 lockdown and their work all came to her. Yet she still took calls from every single one of them daily because they were struggling. Then she worked every waking hour to catch up on her workload. Maybe they felt better after their calls, but she didn't – she couldn't help them and she wasn't helping herself either. As a community we helped her reflect on what that was costing her and how to set some healthier boundaries.

It is a fine line between being supportive and becoming the person that people come to in order to vent. Many of us have a maternal feeling about our teams but they are not children. They are fully formed adults and when we infantalize them by taking on responsibility for their happiness it doesn't serve us or them. If one of your team is unhappy in their role then they need to decide whether to stay and make the best of it or look for another job. Listening to them moan on a weekly basis is not a good use of your time.

You are not responsible for the emotions of your team members. It's not your job to make them happy. It is your job to provide a great working environment to the best of your ability and to be supportive. But only they can be responsible for their own happiness.

As a leader your role involves balancing your team members' needs as individuals and the needs of the organization. If you believe that you have to make people happy in order to be a good leader then you will struggle to say no to them or make tough decisions that impact them. So be caring and a great listener, but make sure that you have resources you can signpost people to if they need additional support such as a Mental Health First Aider or an employee helpline.

 How do I build my credibility as a young manager? See page 199.

Becoming brilliant at delegation

Mastering delegation will make a positive difference to your workload (and your stress levels) and it is essential to being seen as a leader, but many of us find it hard.

We all know that delegation is about effective allocation of resources. For example, there is no point in a CEO spending huge amounts of their time doing admin which many people could do, when no-one else can do the job of CEO. It is also not cost-effective to pay someone a high salary to do tasks that a more junior employee could do.

What most people don't appreciate is that delegation is also a brilliant tool for developing your team members. Delegation is often seen as something that you do *to* someone else, and they don't necessarily enjoy it being done to them. But delegation can provide people with the opportunity to build their skills, gain new experience and have exposure within the organization.

Delegation is also really helpful for succession planning. If you've never delegated anything and you end up leaving your role, then you won't have given anyone the opportunity to be able to easily step into your shoes.

How do you know if you should be delegating more?

- If you are struggling to get through your to-do list.
- If you are lacking time to focus on your own priorities.
- If you spend too much time doing tasks you're not really good at.
- If you are not spending your time focusing on the tasks that only you can do.
- If your team or organization would be completely lost if you left.

The seven deadly sins of delegation

Most managers aren't very good at delegating. A research study by Professor John Hunt at London Business School showed that three out of ten managers thought that they delegated well when in fact only one in ten managers was actually considered good at delegation by the people who worked for them![3] I've identified seven ways in which I often see delegation done badly; I'll share these here, swiftly followed by ways you can remedy these sins.

1. I can do it quicker by myself syndrome

You rarely delegate because by the time you've explained it to someone else, you might as well have done it yourself. This occurs when people are picking the wrong tasks and people, or they're picking a small one-off task, where it probably does take as much time to explain it as it does for someone else to do it.

2. Finding it awkward and uncomfortable to delegate

The mentality behind this is that you feel like you're asking someone to do your work for you. I see this a lot in newly promoted managers, particularly if they've been promoted over their colleagues in the same organization. I also see it in managers who aren't yet fully owning their authority, so they feel uncomfortable asking people to do things. But in fact, delegation can be a great way to develop your team.

3. The control freak

I confess this used to be me and still is sometimes! Control freaks don't delegate because they think no-one else can do it as well as them. And sometimes they're right. *But just because you can do something better than someone else doesn't mean that you are the best person to do it.* If you keep holding on to everything on your to-do list, it will just get bigger, you'll get stuck doing the same old tasks and the people in your team won't get a chance to develop. If you're suffering from this, it is time to give others a chance to develop themselves and to free up your time to focus on more strategic projects. Delegating will help you to progress your career, because instead of just doing the same things, you'll be able to create time and space to think strategically long term and to be more proactive rather than reactive.

4. "They don't do it right"

You tried delegating and were disappointed with the results so now don't trust anyone to do it the right way. This deadly sin is usually due to mismatched expectations – what you were expecting is not what your colleague thought you were expecting, or you've picked the wrong person and project. Using a structured briefing process like the delegation template in your online book resources will help you and your colleague get on the same page and will provide clarity.

You've also got to be careful not to be a disempowering delegator. If you are delegating to someone junior then you will want to explain step by step how you want something done, as well as the final result you want – because they don't have the experience to know the best way to do it. But this is only appropriate for junior colleagues. It is demotivating for senior managers to be told how to do a project that they've been asked to lead on. You need to delegate the authority to decide how to do it, as well as the responsibility for the project. Otherwise they will try and do it your way, which often doesn't come naturally to them (because they aren't you) and everyone feels frustrated.

5. Last minute.com

You run out of time to get everything done so you ask a colleague to help you out. You choose the nearest person (or whoever's got the least on their to-do list right now) and your briefing is rushed. So it isn't really a surprise when it doesn't work out well in that scenario.

6. Partial delegation

You only hand over half the project because the person doesn't have either the skills, knowledge or authority to be able to lead on the whole project. You get frustrated because you keep being asked questions, the project keeps being bouncing back to you and you haven't been able to effectively hand it over. The other person is frustrated because they've got no sense of control or agency over their own work and because they're trying to do something that they can't actually do at all.

7. The boomerang

You delegate the project and it just keeps coming back to you. You have to keep chasing the person to find out what's happening and it never seems to get done, so you end up doing it yourself in the end. That is a sign that you haven't developed your authority yet, because you can be nice, but you still want people to do the work that they have committed to do.

There is one other deadly sin – The dictator – but I doubt this is you if you're reading this book. The dictator doesn't ask someone to do the work; they tell them. And often without warning and at 5pm on a Friday. No-one likes to be on the receiving end of that, which is how delegation gets a bad reputation. And you can probably think back to some of your own experiences of being on the receiving end of a dictator.

The psychology of delegation

If you're guilty of one or two of the deadly sins then understanding the psychology of delegating will help you to understand what's behind your behavior and how to change it to become brilliant at delegating.

If you think back to what you learned in Chapter 2 about mastering your mindset, you'll know that how you think about delegating will determine how you delegate and the results that you get. For example, if you believe that no-one can do it as well as you, then delegation will feel pointless and a waste of your time. So you just don't bother delegating, or you delegate less than you could do, or you do it in a half-hearted way. The impact of that is that you have more work to do.

I've identified the commonly held beliefs that hold people back from delegating effectively along with some strategies you can use.

If you think "I can do it quicker myself": If it is a complex and one-off task then, yes, you probably can complete the task in less time than it takes to explain it to someone else. However, if this is a recurring task then you should create a process so that others can follow the step-by-step instructions to do it in the future. It's simple to do – just write down what you are doing step by step or video yourself completing the task. Someone else could then turn that into a written list if you prefer. Then you can pass the process to your team to carry out from then on. I use this throughout my business, and it has saved me huge amounts of time and makes handover to new team members very easy.

If you feel uncomfortable to ask others to do your work: Part of the role of a manager is to be able to delegate effectively and you shouldn't be delegating *your work*; you should be delegating tasks that are more appropriately done at a more junior level than you. You're paid more because you either have a greater skill level or your level of responsibility is higher, and you need to effectively utilize the resources of your organization. Doing your job well involves delegating effectively.

Delegation is also not an evil thing that you do to someone else. For example, if you're going on holiday and you normally go to your heads of department meeting then you could ask a team member to attend that meeting to represent your team in your absence. That's great exposure for them. They get themselves known and can see how things operate at that organizational or departmental level. The more insight they have about what's happening at the level above them, the better prepared they are to step up into that level one day.

You need to shift your mindset because if you delegate, thinking that you're doing it *to* someone else, then the person you delegate to is going to feel like that as well. They are going to pick up on the beliefs that you have around delegation. The new belief that I'd like you to develop is that *delegation is helping you to develop your team.*

> *"Realizing that delegating is not a bad thing that I have to do to people has completely changed how I feel about it. I love developing my team and now I see delegation as a valuable tool I can use to do that. I'm feeling less overwhelmed already." Helen*

If you think "they don't do it right": I see this a lot in time-poor stressed-out managers, and in particular those who like to remain in control as much as possible. And retaining control has its benefits. But as I've mentioned earlier, it makes it hard to develop your career and to develop your team. I am going to show you how to brief your team better by picking the right person, project and time so that your new belief can be *"I briefed my team well and trust them to deliver."* You'll be taking responsibility for briefing them well and trusting them to deliver.

Briefing effectively

Choose a project which:

- Is a distinct project – so that someone has complete responsibility for it from start to finish.
- Doesn't need your input – if you are the only person with the experience, knowledge, or authority to make certain elements happen then that isn't going to work.
- Is time limited with a clear start and end date – if this is an ongoing task that is being delegated then that's adding to their role rather than delegation.

Pick the right person by asking yourself:

- Do they have the necessary skills?
- Do they have the necessary knowledge and experience?
- Do they have the time to do this?
- Do they need any training related to this project or indeed project management?
- Will they take the right approach? For example, if it is a detailed project are you choosing a naturally detailed person?
- Are there any internal politics associated with who you delegate this project to?

■ Are they comfortable asking questions and asking for what they need?

■ Do they have the appropriate level of authority for this project?

Pick the right time:

■ Give as much advance warning as possible.

■ Ask nicely, not demanding and not apologetically.

■ Make sure you are taking the time to really brief them well.

You'll find a briefing template within your online book resources at www.carlamillertraining.com/bookresources.

 How do I stop my team constantly asking me questions? See page 205.

Chapter 4: Top tips

• Remind yourself of your Personal Leadership Brand power words before you go into meetings.

• Put on your Cloak of Authority when you need to feel ready for a challenging conversation.

• Set clear expectations and hold people accountable to them.

• Use the Behavior, Consequence, Action tool to give clear and actionable feedback.

• Remember that setting boundaries is kinder than resenting people for stepping over boundaries they had no idea existed.

Chapter 5

Communicating with clarity

Many of my coaching clients tell me they struggle with speaking up, getting their voice heard and making their point powerfully in large meetings. According to the 2019 *Women in the Workplace* report by McKinsey & Company and LeanIn.org, women get interrupted 50% of the time in meetings and 96% of those interruptions are by men.[1] Yet if we communicate like men we are judged harshly for it so my approach is to find a communication style that is clear, confident and feels authentic to you. In this chapter you'll find a toolkit for dealing with the common challenges we face in meetings, as well as insights on how you can use language powerfully and increase your gravitas.

Mastering meetings

Meetings are where you want to be seen as a leader so let's get you ready to show up right with strategies for increasing your impact in meetings.

Before the meeting

1. Be clear about what you want to get from the meeting. That might be information, a decision, approval or visibility, for example.

2. Be intentional about how you want to be perceived by others during the meeting – remind yourself of the power words that make up your Personal Leadership Brand so that you can filter your communication and really live your brand in the meeting. If you want to be seen as collaborative, for example, you might ask for feedback more often.

3. Go in feeling more powerful by power posing beforehand. In 2018, Dr Amy Cuddy's TED talk on body language popularized the idea of power posing.[2] She shared that your body language impacts how you feel and that holding expansive powerful body positions for at least two minutes makes you feel and act more powerful for the rest of the day. You can pose like Wonder Woman or throw your hands up in the air in a victory pose like you've just passed the finish line of a marathon. I have clients that power pose in the bathroom before a big meeting and swear it makes them feel more in control. Other clients have a power song they listen to before a big meeting or call.

"My director stopped by my desk and asked me to join the director's meeting to talk about my project yesterday. I had ten minutes so instead of going into panic mode I went to the toilet and power posed. I felt confident and calm and presented really well." Kareesa

4. If you've used the coaching tools in Part 1 of the book, you'll be able to consciously leave your Inner Critic outside the front door of the meeting and tune in to your Inner Leader beforehand.

Your Meeting Toolkit

These are some of the common challenges that come up during meetings and my top tips on how to handle them with ease.

If you worry about what to say

Often we rehearse what we want to say in our head before we say it, meaning we're not being present and paying full attention to what's happening around us. Instead, try jotting down one or two bullet points, so that when you have a chance to speak you know the point you want to make.

My favorite way to contribute to a meeting is by asking questions. I learned long ago that if you've asked an intelligent question during a meeting, you'll be seen as an effective contributor to the group. And because you've already said something you are less likely to be randomly called on to contribute later in the meeting.

Questions also work well for people who like to be 100% sure before speaking up. You can ask a question without having any supporting information to hand. It is a way of contributing and adding value that others really appreciate. You can use questions to keep the meeting on track, raise a different perspective or summarize.

Try being the person who joins the dots. The person who watches and listens and sees the themes, or notices when things are going off track. Often everyone is so busy thinking about themselves and their own perspective that they are not seeing the big picture; when you do, others will see you as strategic.

If you're asked for information you don't have

This often feels uncomfortable, but it doesn't need to be. First, make sure that you know what level of information you should have to be able to do your job well. If you are at director level, for example, you won't and shouldn't know the minutiae of activities happening three levels below you. What you should know is how the project is going overall and any key numbers. If you are a project manager then you'll be expected to know the detail of the project you are managing as part of doing your job well, so go armed with your spread-sheets or project plan.

Then be aware of the pet projects of the senior stake-holders in the room. If you know the CEO is really interested in how a certain event or project is going, then go in with that information to hand. If something you lead on is high risk, you can expect interest in the detail of the riskier elements.

Sometimes you'll work with a person who is all about the detail. It isn't a great use of your time to spend hours prepping for meetings with them or living in fear of being asked for infor-mation you don't have to hand. If you believe that doing your job well does not mean knowing that information immediately, then try this sentence which is responsive but unapologetic:

"I can certainly gather that information… I'll get that to you tomorrow/this afternoon."

If you are a reflective thinker

About a third of us are introverts, which means we are likely to have a more reflective thinking style. Unfortunately, meetings are designed around extroverted thinking styles. They often demand quick decisions and immediate answers.

"Meetings are a nightmare for me. As an introvert I like to reflect before speaking and I dread being put on the spot. Then I beat myself up for not contributing enough to meetings." Emilia

Often introverts end up embarrassed of their thinking style or seeing it as a weakness. But it is not a weakness; it's just that meetings rarely accommodate reflective time. Here's what you can do:

1. **Own it**. As with any point of difference, you can choose to compare yourself unfavorably to others, or you can be proud of it and position it as a strength. Reflective thinking where all options are carefully considered is an asset to your team and organization and diversity in any form, including thinking styles, improves team performance.

2. **Change the way meetings work**. Introduce better agendas, with key background information and decisions that need to be made, and circulate them before the meeting to allow reflective thinkers to come in prepared. Allow time in the meeting for reflection. You could even change meetings so that they are split into two parts held on separate days, one to discuss and one to make a final decision.

3. **Talk to your manager**. Make sure your manager and other key stakeholders know that you have a reflective thinking style and how to get the best from you.

If you want to buy yourself some thinking time, try:

"Great question… let me give it some thought and come back to you tomorrow."

If you are being pressed for an immediate answer:

"If you need an answer now I'd say… but I'd like to think through the implications (adapt as relevant) *and come back to you."*

If you feel like you talk too much in meetings

The extroverts I coach sometimes regret talking so much in meetings and question the value of their contribution. But remember, meetings don't work if no-one talks! If you feel that you contribute too much, try waiting for at least two people to contribute before you do. Notice if you interrupt, apologize, and let the other person finish. Try jotting down your point instead so you don't forget it. Interrupting can cause people to feel that their contribution isn't valued, even if in fact you were super inspired by it.

If you're the one being interrupted

This can be tricky to deal with because you don't want to create tension – people will recall the tension rather than your valuable contribution. You've got to judge the strength of your response on the moment, the seniority of the person involved, and whether they are a serial interrupter. There are cultural differences too – I see women in the States being much more assertive around challenging interruptions than their British counterparts.

If someone is trying to interrupt you but you want to finish your point, try *"Almost finished…"* or *"One moment…,"* possibly supported by holding up your hand to indicate you haven't finished speaking.

If this is a serial interrupter you could go bolder with *"I'd like to finish my point…"* or *"I'm still talking…"*

If you were interrupted but still want to make your point you could use *"Yes and…"* or *"As I was saying…"*

You might also want to work with the other women in the room to champion each other. This is something that the women in Obama's inner circle who had to fight to be heard called amplification.[3] It involved helping other women in the room be heard by repeating their key point and giving them credit for it so the men in the room could not take the credit. You can use phrases like *"Monique was interrupted and I'd like to hear the rest of Monique's point"* or *"I thought Monique's point was really interesting, could you tell us more please Monique?"*

Using powerful language

If you start listening out for it in meetings, you'll soon notice some phrases that only the women in the room use when they start their contribution. I call these caveats.

Caveats sound like:

"I might be wrong but…"
"I'm not sure but…"
"Sorry…"
"I just…"
"This might be a waste of time but…"

We want to make a point, but think we might be judged in some way for making it and so caveat it in the hope that we can avoid conflict or judgment. Often using these phrases then becomes a habit which we apply to our general speech.

It's a survival mechanism because at some level we don't feel entirely safe speaking up in meetings. This might be due to personal past experiences, or a concept known as "Patriarchy Stress Disorder," where we are reacting to the ancestral and collective trauma experienced by women in the patriarchal world for millennia. According to Dr Valerie Rein, the author of the book *Patriarchy Stress Disorder*,[4] it has never been safe for women to speak up, even for recent generations of women, and that validated fear has been passed down through generations of women.

What each of these caveats essentially says is *"What I'm about to say probably isn't worth listening to."* Which is of course precisely the opposite of what we want to communicate!

> *"I don't think I'm wrong, I am sure about my facts and I'm not actually sorry either. So why do I use those phrases?"* Sue

We are giving away our power without realizing it by using these phrases, criticizing ourselves before others have the chance to do it. Women are more harshly judged for their input than men are, so how do we raise points that could be seen as challenging without being unlikable?

I'm a big fan of using questions to make a point. As long as your tone is right, a question which makes your point means you come across as both insightful and welcoming the contributions of others. Of course, sometimes you just need to make your point directly to be heard. Here are some of my favorite opening questions and statements to use:

"Have we considered all the options?"
"I wonder if…?"
"How about?"
"What if…?"
"Is there a reason we're not considering…?
"We could also look at this another way…"
"In my experience…"

As well as starting strong we want to end strong as well. Uncomfortable in the spotlight, I used to end my contribution to a large meeting with a shrug that clearly said *"Please move on to the next person now as I don't like everyone looking at me."* I often see that shrug in meeting rooms, or the tailing off of a sentence as you realize you don't know how to finish strong. I also often hear:

"Does that make sense?"
"But maybe I'm wrong"
"That's all from me"

I've coached an extremely accomplished leader, who when outside of her comfort zone finishes most of her contributions by saying *"Does that make sense?"*. She *knows* it makes sense. What she is doing is constantly looking for validation that she deserves to contribute and is adding value. Now that she understands this, she has dropped that phrase and communicates powerfully.

There is a time and place for the phrase *"Does that make sense?"*. If you've just explained something complicated or if you are checking that someone has understood your instructions it can be a useful phrase. But as a default ending to your meeting contributions, it's a poor phrase to use.

As a side note, personally I don't think the word *"sorry"* should be removed from our vocabulary. In fact, as someone who is naturally direct in my speech, I sometimes strategically use it to soften the blow of the point I'm about to make. It can be a useful strategy for anyone who is called direct or aggressive. And with some unpleasant personalities it can be unsafe to challenge their points directly, so you may want to use a caveat like that. And of course sometimes we do actually need to apologize!

To end strong, once you've made your final point, imagine a full stop at the end of your sentence and take a breath. That tells people you have finished. Make eye contact with others in the room and sit back or bring your hands together to indicate that you've now made your point. Anything is better than that "stop looking at me" shrug. Try and sit with the attention of the room for just a moment longer – it's key to being visible and building your career. And if you want feedback try using phrases such as

"Any questions?"

"Any reflections on that?"

Having gravitas

The last piece in being seen as a leader is gravitas, which is defined as dignity, seriousness, or being solemn of nature.

Clients have come to me because they've been told that they need to have more gravitas. When I dig a bit deeper, they've been told by their male manager or their chief executive that they are "too smiley" or "too friendly" or "too nice" to be taken seriously at the next level of leadership. One woman was even called too "fluffy," which is pretty outrageous given a man would never be called fluffy!

I completely dispute the idea that if your default is to be smiley and friendly, you cannot be taken seriously as a leader. I don't think you have to completely change your personality in order to be taken seriously as a leader. But you do need to be able to step into the authority that comes with your role, as I covered earlier.

Gravitas used to be an everyday requirement for leadership. In the 1980s and well into the 90s, a manager and a leader was someone (usually a man in a gray suit) who told you what to do. It was a very directive, authoritarian style of management, often with an element of fear – a style that thankfully we don't come across too often now. Leadership has evolved since then. And women no longer need to act like old men in gray suits to be taken seriously as leaders. But there are times when we do have to deliver serious news or address a roomful of people who intimidate us. And that is where gravitas comes in.

Many years ago, I undertook a day of media training alongside the other directors at the children's charity I worked for. It was one of those days where you go and practice dealing with radio and TV interviews around a crisis situation. We were all videoed giving an interview and reading a statement on television about a (fictional) really serious accusation that had been lodged against a staff member.

What I realized from watching the video played back was that while I was communicating well in terms of content, I had zero gravitas. I was about 30 years old and I came across as a very sweet, earnest person who was out of their depth. Unlike my CEO who had perfected her tone of voice for such scenarios, my tone of voice was just my normal tone, which was friendly. It was really clear that should we have a situation like that I was not going to be the obvious spokesperson.

Let's address the fact that when it comes to gravitas, women are at a disadvantage. The physical traits that convey gravitas such as having a deeper voice and a larger stature are all masculine ones.

It's been proven that the lower your voice, the more seriously you're taken, and the more people sit up and listen. There was a presenter of the *Today* program on Radio 4 here in the UK who shared that when they are delivering serious news, they lower their voice because it triggers something in people where they think "this is serious, I better listen to this."[5]

The main reason we need gravitas is when we need to reflect, or need someone to understand, the seriousness of the situation. Such as in crisis situations like the scenario I outlined above. But we also need it in performance management conversations where someone needs to improve to keep their job, when dealing with redundancies and when dealing with bullying or discrimination.

You may also want more gravitas in a situation that intimidates you or where you are surrounded by older men who may be likely to underestimate you.

Interviews can also be a time to dial up the gravitas a bit. You don't want to become a completely different person but if you think you may not be taken seriously at that level, you can purposefully share times when you've had to make tough decisions or communicate serious news so that they can picture you doing that in the role.

So how do you increase your gravitas?

- Ground yourself
  Grounding yourself means putting your feet flat on the floor, which makes you more solid and stable. When you want gravitas, you don't want to seem like if someone pushes you, metaphorically you will fall over. Imagine yourself as an oak tree and when you put your feet on the ground there are roots going from your feet deep into the earth.

- Stand (or sit) tall
  If you are standing up, make sure that your weight is equally distributed between your hips. Women often stand with their weight on one side and this doesn't add to our physical stature. If you are a natural slumper then focus on sitting up straight with your shoulders back. You don't need to be like those men that take up as much space as physically possible but you want to claim your space.

- Don't fidget
  If you are constantly fidgeting or moving around it makes you appear nervous. If, like me, you struggle to stay still

for a long time, find a way to move that isn't as visible, e.g., under the table. If you know you fiddle with jewelry like necklaces then avoid wearing them when you need gravitas.

- Speak from the diaphragm
A lower tone helps you to make more impact on your listeners and conveys authority. Caroline Goyder has fantastic tips on using your voice within her book *Gravitas*.[6] One of them is to take your thumb and massage the spot where your ribs separate at the front of your body (just underneath the front of your bra strap). You'll notice that your voice deepens slightly and that's the tone you are aiming for.

- Slow down
The faster you speak, the harder it is to have authority and gravitas. I speak quickly when I'm nervous. I think a lot of us do because we're not comfortable taking up lots of space in the conversation. We think that we need to make our point as quickly as possible and get it over with so that other people can go back to talking. But you want to speak more slowly when you're communicating that serious news. The simplest way to do that is to use shorter sentences, pause between those sentences, and close your mouth when you pause.

- Get comfortable with silences, even awkward ones
Silence is powerful. It can help your point to land. It can convey that what was said wasn't acceptable. It's not your

job to make everyone feel comfortable. That's a big task to take on and there are times when you *want* someone to feel uncomfortable. It's never okay to make someone feel unvalued or disrespected, but if someone is not putting in any effort at work you don't want to make them feel that is fine – you want them to know that it isn't acceptable and needs to change.

Chapter 5: Top tips

- Power pose for two minutes before a big meeting to feel more powerful.

- Notice how you start and end your contribution to meetings and try out some of the phrases from the Meeting Toolkit.

- Get together with some other women in your organization and agree to amplify each other's voices in meetings.

- Try using questions instead of making statements.

- Use your body language to increase your gravitas by placing your feet flat on the floor and sitting up straight.

- Slow down and lower your tone for increased gravitas.

Part 3

Increasing your influence and impact

You've done the inner work and taken steps to be seen as a leader, so now you have laid the foundations to successfully influence sideways and upwards. In Part 3 we will be building up your influencing skills with practical coaching tools, useful insights into what may be holding you back as an influencer and, of course, the steps you can take to close the Influence Gap and get your voice heard.

We'll be looking at your relationship with your manager, how to successfully navigate internal politics, and how to speak the language of senior stakeholders.

Chapter 6 – Navigating internal politics
Learn how to lay the foundations of influencing by building strategic relationships, using my six-step model for influencing and noticing how you may be getting in your own way.

Chapter 7 – Influencing senior stakeholders
There is a skill to managing upwards and that is what you're going to learn in this chapter, from partnering with your line manager to speaking the language of senior stakeholders.

Navigating internal politics

Before I understood influencing, I used to hate what I called "internal politics," but now I see the importance of strategic relationship building so that my team can succeed and I enjoy it. Here's how you can look at it differently too and how you can think like a leader when operating internally.

Strategic relationship building

This starts with identifying who can help your team to succeed and where tensions might arise between your team and others. Then you can invest time in those relationships to improve them. I encourage you to ask yourself these questions:

1. Who does my team rely on for the resources we need? How do I want that person or team to perceive me? What can I do to make it easier for them to help me?
2. Where are there tensions between my team and others? How much time is it costing me to deal with these tensions? What could I do to proactively address these issues with my peers?

What you will be doing is building your team's personal brand – taking control of how your team is perceived by others within the organization.

Then you can apply the principles in the model below to build your relationship with these stakeholders so that you are giving your team the best chance of success.

 How do I deal with tension between my team and another team? See page 203.

 ## Coaching tool: A six-step model for influencing

There are some simple but powerful steps that you can take to enable you to influence anyone – from team members to senior stakeholders – and I've pulled them into a six-step model for you.

Step 1 – Build your relationship

If someone knows and likes you then they will be more likely to sit down and discuss issues with you, listen properly and recognize your positive intentions. And your rapport will be much better. So invest time in getting to know them, asking after their hobbies, family etc., and checking in on them if they look like they are having a hard time. Genuinely care about them as a person.

Step 2 – Understand them

To be able to influence someone you need to be able to look at the situation from their perspective (and it might even change your perspective). This step is about putting your-self in their shoes. What are their priorities? What do they get excited about? What do they worry about? What makes them feel valued? What do they focus on – big picture or detail? You can use the perspectives coaching tool later in this chapter for some great insight to help you with this.

Step 3 – Establish what they want from the situation

Ideally you'd be having conversations to establish this and asking lots of great questions. If that isn't possible then put yourself back in their shoes and think about what they want from the situation. What might they be concerned about? What most interests them? Where does this fit on their list of priorities? Is this important to their key stakeholders? Is this situation going to impact their career development or the status of their team?

Step 4 – Know what you want

While it would be brilliant if we got everything we wanted, sometimes we can lose out on getting a yes because of one small sticking point that isn't that important to us. So think about the elements of what you are proposing that really matter and the ones that are "nice to haves" rather than "need to haves."

Step 5 – Acknowledge their needs/priorities/concerns and share yours

Most people attempt to influence while only seeing things from their own perspective. They may even blame the other person for the issue, which leads to tension and frustration.

Conversely, this model encourages you to think like a leader and see the situation from a different perspective. When you acknowledge the other person's needs, priorities or concerns, it sets a different, solution-focused tone of mutual respect. Other people will find it refreshing and most will respond in turn. And when you share your needs, priorities or concerns, you are being straightforward and putting your needs on an equal footing with theirs.

Step 6 – Suggest a solution that meets both of your needs as a starting point for discussion

Create a solution that, based on what you know, could potentially work for both parties. You can then propose it as a starting point for discussion, not a fait accompli. Together you can iron out the issues and navigate toward an outcome that you can both take ownership of. This isn't about you or them compromising; it is about you both winning. Focus your communication on highlighting how what you propose is beneficial to them, drawing on what you know is important to them.

If you are dealing with someone that you know drives a hard bargain or won't compromise then you can talk through how your solution is preferable to the current stalemate and use the tips about unconscious habits later in this chapter to persuade them. Your position isn't one of weakness; it's one of leadership and thinking about what is best for the organization.

When to use this model

You can use this approach both within a single conversation or an ongoing negotiation.

Within a single conversation it might look like this:

Step 1: "How was your weekend?"

Step 2: "What are you and your team working on at the moment?"

Step 3: "What is your thinking on X at the moment? What would you like to leave this discussion with? Do you have any concerns about X?"

Step 4: Think about their answers and also what is most important for you in the context of this discussion.

Step 5: "I hear that X is a concern for you and that you've got some competing priorities. From my perspective I'm trying to balance X with Y and so Z is important to be able to achieve that."

Step 6: "Bearing all of that in mind, shall we think of some solutions that work for both of us? How about…?"

Within an ongoing negotiation it might look like this:

Step 1: Investing time getting to know your colleague in a call or over coffee.

Step 2: Mapping out in your head where this fits in their list of priorities, how they like to receive information and listening to the questions they ask.

Step 3: Listening carefully to their concerns and objections and delving deeper to really understand what is driving those.

Step 4:   Thinking about what you want and possible points of
            tension and solutions that work for all involved.
Steps 5 and 6: Having a meeting where you discuss the key
            points of the negotiation, both coming with an open
            mind to create a solution that works for everyone.

I have also used this approach successfully in overall
relationships with key stakeholders. When I was an interim
fundraising director, whenever I started in a new assignment
I would identify the people that my team and I needed to
work closely with. In most of the charities I'd worked in over
the years there was tension between the Fundraising team
and two other teams – Finance and Programs – because
they were interdependent. In my first week I would arrange
coffees with my peers that led those teams. I'd spend a third
of the chat getting to know them personally (hobbies, family,
background, etc.), a third of the chat getting their take on the
best way to get things done within the organization, and then
the final third asking how our teams worked together and
what they'd like to be different.

At the same time, I'd also be getting to know my team
and hearing their thoughts on the relationships with the other
teams. Once I had the complete picture, I'd spend some time
thinking about better ways of working and then arrange a
one-hour meeting with the relevant director to chat through
how we could improve the ways our teams worked together.
It was really refreshing for them to feel understood, and it
started our relationship off on the right foot. When tensions
did arise we problem-solved them together without a blame
culture.

Once you are at head of team level, navigating internally isn't a distraction from your job; it's a major part of your job – smoothing the way for your team and ironing out issues. And if you focus on helping your team to succeed, while applying the mindset shifts below, you will soon be standing out as a leader and that will help you to develop your career.

Thinking like a leader

There are certain mindset shifts that you can make which will make it easier to navigate internally and increase your influence and impact. I call this thinking like a leader, and I developed these mindset shifts after noticing what worked for me, observing what worked for others, applying personal development techniques to a leadership context and sharing them with coaching clients over the years.

Take radical responsibility

When I started implementing this mindset shift, I quickly became seen as a leader. *Radical responsibility means you stop complaining about problems and start solving them instead. As a leader you have the ability to make change happen, even when it is outside of your job description.*

When I was working at Samaritans as the head of one of five fundraising teams, I noticed that we were not getting the information we needed from Finance to be able to track funds effectively. It was one of those things we moaned about in team meetings. I got bored of moaning and collated all of our issues and needs and set up a meeting with a colleague in the Finance team. I explained what we needed and why and talked through the issues while also asking for their perspective on the issue. Together we came up with a better system that worked for both departments and we didn't waste time moaning about it anymore.

I took this approach on a number of issues and when my maternity cover contract came to an end my director didn't want me to leave and I was promoted to interim Head of Fundraising – a new position. I also took this approach when I worked at Charity People, which resulted in me being made managing director within a year. On neither occasion was I aiming for a promotion; I was trying to make it easier for me and my team to do our jobs well. I can spot problems and come up with solutions naturally.

If there is an issue you constantly complain about, you could probably benefit from taking radical responsibility for it. That doesn't mean doing all the work – sometimes it is about raising it with a senior stakeholder or offering to coordinate a working group.

> *"I started taking radical responsibility into action whenever I felt frustrated and suddenly I'm on the radar of my CEO. Last week he asked me to be a case study for a PR initiative highlighting strong women leaders in the business whilst 6 months ago my manager told me I needed to develop my leadership skills." Abigail*

Focus on possibility, not problems

As a leader of your team but also within your organization, you set the tone for the discussions you have. It can be easy to get pulled down into group negativity, particularly when times are tough but there is a difference between acknowledging emotions and challenges and dwelling on them. If you are the person focusing on possibility rather than problems you can help others to feel more positive too. My own coach says *"A leader is someone who can see the future that others cannot yet see and guides them towards it"* and I love that approach. I like to take a "can-do" attitude. Recognize challenges and issues but encourage your team to focus on what they can control using questions to channel them such as *"What can we do to be part of the solution or inspire change?"* or pointing out that talking about the problems makes us feel frustrated, while focusing on solutions makes us feel a better sense of control.

How you are BEING is as important as what you are DOING

Much leadership training focuses on what you are DOING, but in fact how you are BEING is just as important. People will respond to your energy. I set an intention to make people's day better for having spent time with me rather than worse. That way, people will want to spend time with you, even if it is to discuss challenging issues. You can't influence anyone if they avoid talking to you.

Make your team bigger

No, I'm not talking about empire building here! Instead of seeing it as your team against the world, treat your peers as if you are on the same team. Celebrate their successes, understand their priorities, advocate for them and look for the win-win when tensions arise. It will make a refreshing change for them and they will want to work with you.

Building trust

As well as implementing the mindset shifts above, there are some foundational steps you can take to gain the trust and respect of your peers – which is crucial when influencing:

- **Do what you say you'll do.** It can be tempting to say yes to everything to please other people. But when you say yes to everything and are overcommitted, you disappoint people by letting them down. To gain respect they need to trust that you will do what you say you'll do – on time and to a good standard. If you can't deliver on that, you won't be able to influence anyone as that fundamental trust won't be there.

- **Admit when you've made a mistake.** We all make mistakes sometimes and it is so refreshing when someone owns their mistakes, apologizes and does what they can to rectify it. Many organizations have a blame culture, which you can help to break by admitting when you've made a mistake without beating yourself up for being human. Admitting mistakes is about taking responsibility, even if the mistake was by omission or was the best you could do at the time.

- **Be generous about giving credit to others.** I've always said the worst kind of manager takes credit for work that someone else did (this happened to me a lot earlier on in my career). The opposite of that is to thank colleagues for their contribution to your successes and make sure that they are credited for the work they put in. You can create a monthly report for your team which acts as an influencing tool by keeping others informed about what your team is doing, showing all the work that is going on, and also publicly thanking any colleagues who have been instrumental to the successes. If someone is helping you, be sure to let them know the outcome personally and thank them for the part they played in it too.

- **Treat people as you'd like to be treated.** If you'd like others to give you positive feedback and advocate for your team and champion you, then you can start by doing that for them.

How we get in our own way when it comes to influencing

When we are trying to influence others, we often make them the problem. They're difficult to deal with. They won't listen. They don't understand. Yet in fact we are often getting in our own way when it comes to influencing and exacerbate the situation, causing more tension. I'm going to teach you how you can stop doing that and start showing up differently by responding rather than reacting, using a coaching tool to see things from the other person's perspective.

Are you reacting or responding?

When a comment, situation or experience triggers us, we can find ourselves reacting rather than responding. Our freeze, fight or flight instinct kicks in and we may find ourselves going red, snapping defensively, getting high pitched in our tone or withdrawing from the conversation altogether. None of those reactions improve the situation or add to our credibility, and some make it worse.

What we want to do is to calmly respond, having thought through what we are trying to achieve with our response. That is how we influence others. We might choose to respond by setting a boundary, sharing an alternative perspective or tabling the discussion for a later date when we've had time to reflect.

Michelle, a PR manager in a construction firm, felt wronged by her manager. She wanted to call her manager and rant at her about how unfair the situation was. I asked her *"What do you hope to achieve by that? What impact do you think it will have?"* As she reflected, she realized that while part of her wanted to express her feelings, it wasn't going to land well or improve the situation. Together we established the outcome she wanted from the conversation and a way to get that while also sharing honest feedback with her manager on the impact of their actions. She moved from reacting strongly to responding powerfully.

How do we get better at responding rather than reacting? According to neuroscientist Dr Jill Bolte-Taylor, when we are triggered our bodies are flooded by emotions and hormones for 90 seconds.[1] During those 90 seconds you will find it hard to respond calmly so here are some tips:

- Notice you are reacting (you can get to know the unique way you respond when triggered).

- Use a holding sentence like *"Let me think about that for a moment"* while you take a couple of subtle deep breaths and ground yourself by noticing your feet on the floor.
- Ask yourself if your reaction is reasonable – this will help you determine your response.
- Think about what you want to achieve with your response.

As a side note, once those 90 seconds are up, you will no longer be flooded by hormones. But if you replay the incident in your head then you will be flooded by hormones once again as your brain thinks it is real. So set it aside once you've responded rather than dwelling on it for the rest of the meeting or day.

There's no judgment here for reacting. We all have triggers and we all react. What you want to be able to do is recognize it, check if your reaction is reasonable and decide how you want to respond. This is a lifelong skill to develop and one which is helpful outside of the workplace too.

Some situations rightly trigger a reaction. Being the victim of, or witnessing, discrimination or abuse of power quite rightly triggers an angry reaction in us. But you still want to be able to respond calmly and powerfully in the way you challenge such behavior.

However, discrimination excepted, often we are triggered because we are getting in our own way and that is what I'd like to help you avoid.

What triggers us?

1. Our unspoken rules have been broken

We each carry around in our heads a rule book about how people should or shouldn't act. When someone breaks one of our rules we get annoyed and judge them as wrong. The thing is, everyone's rule book is different and other people don't know what your unspoken rules are. Some people think it is rude to have your camera off on a video call; others think it is good for their wellbeing. Some people like to take notes on their phone during a meeting; others think that means those people are not listening. Rules crop up around timeliness, email signoffs, the use of technology, interrupting and much more.

If you find yourself triggered because a rule has been broken, you can remind yourself that not everyone shares your rule book and in fact some people hold precisely the opposite rule. You can choose to stop judging them as wrong or disrespectful and you'll find yourself less triggered. You can even proactively identify your rules and question them – in my Influence & Impact course I ask members to share their rules within breakout rooms so that they can see that some perfectly reasonable and lovely people don't agree with all of their rules.

If you're a team leader, you might want to collectively set some guidelines (people don't like the word "rules") with your team on how you want to treat each other, show up at meetings, and so on, if this is an area that is causing tension.

2. Our values are being stepped on

Your values are what are important to you and often determine your behavior. It's helpful to know your values as part of thinking about the sort of leader you want to be. But sometimes we hold our values too tightly or define them too narrowly, which can cause issues.

Feeling like our values are being stepped on can really trigger us. If we believe that someone is doing something fundamentally wrong, then one of our values has probably been stepped on.

Ellie, who headed up a Customer Service team in a software business, held honesty as a huge value of hers. One of the ways she translated honesty was as transparency, and she wanted to be more transparent with customers about some areas of the organization's plans. This request was denied by the chief technology officer as he felt it would be taking an unnecessary risk.

But because honesty was so important to her and she translated it as transparency, Ellie believed that the CTO was being less than honest. She started to feel misaligned with the values of the organization. Yet I'm sure the CTO was a decent person who did share her value of honesty; he just did not think transparency and honesty were the same thing. Through coaching Ellie recognized that she was triggered and that his point was a valid one, and she went back with a stronger business case.

My advice is to know your values and make sure your employer's values are aligned with those, but also recognize that everyone holds different values (and in a different order) and translates them differently. If I asked you and three other readers to write me a definition of honesty, for example, they would all be slightly different.

3. Our unconscious needs are keeping us stuck

A coach I once worked with introduced me to the concept of unconscious addictions and how they cause tension in relationships. I prefer the term unconscious needs, but they are useful to understand and recognize when they come up. We each experience at least one, if not all, of these and they can cause us to become very entrenched and inflexible in our dealings with others. In the same way as we put our Inner Critics in the backseat in Part 1 of this book, we want to be able to recognize when our unconscious needs are doing the driving because they will impact our ability to be rational and influence effectively.

Unconscious need	The negative impact	Things to try
The need to be right	Makes it hard to see things from alternative perspectives	Ask yourself – would I rather be right or happy?
The need to look good	Makes us afraid to admit mistakes	Embrace a growth mindset and see failure as useful information
The need for safety	Makes us too risk-averse	Consciously look for the upside as well as the risk

The need for control	Makes it hard to delegate or trust our teams	Read Chapter 4 on leading with confidence to work on your beliefs
The need to be liked	Makes it hard to have difficult conversations	Read Chapter 4 for information on leading your team

The other way in which we make it harder for ourselves to influence is by thinking there is only one way to look at the situation. That is where the perspectives coaching tool can come in very handy.

Coaching tool: Seeing things from a different perspective

When it comes to influencing, the ability to recognize and appreciate other perspectives is crucial. To be able to influence someone, you need to be able to see the situation from their perspective and to put yourself in their shoes. Not only will that enable you to speak to what it is important to them, it also enriches your understanding of the situation and may even change your perspective.

What's your perspective?

We see the world through a filter of our own experiences, the model of the world we have built up in our minds, our emotions and the information we have access to. This means we can look at exactly the same situation as someone else and see it differently.

You and I could have a conversation and take totally different things away from that conversation because our minds focused on different aspects and tuned out different things, and we were feeling different emotions.

The illustration below is a classic example – both people are looking at the same thing but from different perspectives – and they are both right and wrong!

The best leaders have developed cognitive flexibility – the ability to take perspectives very different to your own and to suspend judgment and see a different side to the issue before you make the decision. These leaders recognize that their view is just one perspective and that other perspectives can add value to decision making.

It isn't always easy to see things from a different perspective, particularly if we feel strongly about something. This exercise can help you to practice that – for maximum effect, move around the room as you try on the different perspectives – it will enable you to look at things differently.

First, I'll share with you an example of how a client used this coaching exercise and then I will talk you through how you can use it.

Sophia was experiencing a lot of tension with her manager, who she felt did not listen to her or value her opinion. From her perspective, she felt he was often dismissive and unsupportive.

I encouraged her to put herself in his shoes and think about how he might describe the situation and her behavior. It took a while to reflect on that, but she decided he probably had no idea that she was feeling unvalued, that he didn't know how to support her and found her behavior defensive at times.

Then I asked Sophia to imagine she was in a helicopter as a neutral observer looking down at the situation and asked her what she saw. She saw two people with conflicting communication styles who both had good intentions and were not communicating their needs or listening to each other well.

After looking at the situation from all three perspectives, Sophia decided she would clearly ask for the support she needed and she would give her manager the benefit of the doubt by focusing on his good intentions rather than assuming he did not value her. This would also help her to be less defensive in her communication with him.

Let's get you applying this tool now. Before you start:

- Grab a pen and piece of paper.
- Think of a situation where you have tension with somebody else.
- Place two chairs opposite each other with an object in between them which represents the situation (it could be any object at all).

1. Look at the situation from *your* perspective

Sit in the chair you feel drawn to first, look at the object that represents the situation and write down on your piece of paper how you really feel about this situation and person. How would you describe the situation? How would you describe their approach and behavior?

2. Look at the situation from *their* perspective

Move to the other chair and imagine stepping into their shoes as you look at the situation (represented by the object you chose earlier) from a different angle. How might the other person describe it? How might they describe your approach and behavior? Write down what comes to you. This may be hard if you've never put yourself in their shoes before or if you are very entrenched in being right, but keep trying.

3. Look at the situation from an *observer's* perspective

Step back where you can see both chairs and reflect on the situation as a neutral observer. You might want to imagine you have gone up in a helicopter and are looking down on the situation objectively from a distance. How would an observer describe this situation? How would they describe the behaviors they see?

4. Reflect

What insights have you gained from this exercise?

What could you do to improve this relationship or situation?

Once you have done this for a few situations, your mind will get used to considering situations from the other person's perspective and an observer's perspective. This will make you a more powerful influencer and a more skilled manager and leader.

 How can I influence when working virtually?
See page 201.

Chapter 6: Top tips

- Identify the people who impact your team's ability to deliver and start implementing the six-step model for influencing by building your relationship with them.

- To stand out as a leader, start thinking like a leader and take radical responsibility.

- Remember to respond rather than react and don't keep replaying situations in your head as your brain will react all over again.

- If you are struggling to influence somebody, try the perspectives exercise to see things from their point of view.

Chapter 7

Influencing senior stakeholders

Nothing is quite as nerve-wracking as presenting to senior stakeholders, so in this chapter I'm going to teach you how to speak their language so you can get your voice heard and your value recognized. First though, let's explore possibly the most crucial working relationship you have – the one with your manager.

Often you won't be able to influence senior stakeholders directly and will need to influence them through your manager, so having a solid relationship with your manager is an important part of influencing effectively.

Building your relationship with your manager

The best relationships with managers are more like partnerships, where both parties are there to enable the other to do their job well and are supportive of each other. We often have huge expectations of our manager, which can be hard to live up to when operating in an imperfect world without the time and resources they'd like to be able to give us. These are my top tips on what you can do to create a great working relationship with your manager:

1. See part of your role as helping them to succeed – this mindset shift is how leaders think. Understand their priorities, recognize the pressure they are under and ask what you can do to help. If they feel like you are a team, they will share more with you. This will give you a better insight into how the wider organization functions, providing information that will enable you to influence more effectively.

2. Ask how they are doing – check in with them and see how they are doing. They have feelings, a life outside of work and things on their to-do list that they don't want to do too. Ask after their family, pets, hobbies etc.

3. Be clear on what you need and ask for it – my client Jane was unhappy because her manager wasn't supporting her enough. I asked her *"What support do you need?"* and *"Have you actually asked for it?"* and she realized that she wasn't clear on what support she wanted and hadn't asked for it. Telling your manager you feel "unsupported" doesn't help them to support you better. If you need regular feedback, more encouragement, more access to senior stakeholders or for your meetings to not be cancelled regularly, then ask for that and explain why it is important to you. You may not get it but at least you have asked clearly.

4. Accept that they are human too – which means they will make mistakes, may not be able to meet all of your needs and may not always communicate as you'd like them to. None of us are perfect and we

often hold our managers to higher standards than
we hold ourselves to. This is particularly important
if you think and communicate in a different way to
your manager as that will lead to tensions.

5. Recognize their strengths – you may work for
   someone who has less experience in your area than
   you do or who thinks differently from you, but try
   and recognize what they do well and what they
   contribute.

6. See any tension between you as an interpersonal
   issue rather than making them wrong – it helps to
   focus your frustration on the relationship rather than
   the person. If you see someone as wrong or a bad
   person, you'll find it very hard to see things from their
   perspective and influence them.

7. If at first you don't succeed, try again – if you don't
   get what you need or the answer you want, find out
   what would need to change for that to happen. A
   "no" may not be a "no" next time if circumstances
   have changed.

 How do I improve my relationship with my
manager? See page 207.

 ## Coaching tool: Giving feedback upwards

In Part 2, I shared the Behavior, Consequences, Action feedback tool, which works very effectively with direct reports.
When you are giving feedback upwards or sideways, you
need to take a more nuanced approach which focuses on

the situation rather than the individual, so I developed this simple tool to give you a structure for doing that.

Situation – this is the situation which is causing issues
Consequence – this is why it is a problem
Solution – this is what we could do differently
Outcome – this is the outcome we hope to be closer to reaching

Using the tool sideways could look like this:

Situation: *"I've noticed a lot of tension between our teams."*
Consequence: *"I'm finding myself drawn into conversations that shouldn't need me involved and I'm sure you are finding the same. This isn't an efficient use of our time."*
Solution: *"Shall we each consult with our teams and then spend 30 minutes together identifying the problems and coming up with long-term solutions to them instead of firefighting as they come up?"*
Outcome: *"It would be great to give our teams the clarity they need, iron out the issues and remove the need for us to get involved."*
Using the tool upwards could look like this:

Situation: *"You asked Sunita in my team to carry out some work for you last week."*
Consequence: *"Because it didn't come through me, she didn't know where it sat within her priorities and so she prioritized it over a key project and we almost missed a crucial deadline that impacts X project."*
Solution: *"Going forward please, could you delegate projects through me?"*
Outcome: *"That would allow me to make the best use of the team's resources and ensure we don't miss any crucial deadlines. Thanks."*

Disagreeing with someone more senior than you

There will be times when doing your job well requires you to disagree with someone more senior than you. Many of us have never learned how to effectively and constructively challenge people in senior positions. This can, in fact, be a brilliant way to build your relationship and credibility if you do it well so let's explore how to do that.

I've been on my own journey of learning how to disagree with or challenge someone with authority. As a youngster I hated people abusing their authority and would call them out on it. I wasn't always popular with my teachers because instead of challenging their behavior, what I was actually doing was challenging their *authority*. And that is rarely a helpful thing to do.

When I coach people, I find that they tend to fall into two camps on this issue.

Camp 1 – you never say no to people who are more senior than you. You say yes to everything, no matter the implications for you and your team. You feel very uncomfortable challenging the thinking of someone more senior than you.

Camp 2 – you are frequently challenging authority, but that's not really working for you. It is leading to tension in your relationships and damaging your personal brand (and potentially your career too) because you're not doing it in quite the right way.

Either of those resonate? If so, don't feel bad – this is a skill we rarely get taught.

There is an unspoken and outdated rule that you have to say yes to everything that someone more senior asks of you. Yes to all the extra work. Yes to the projects that you actually think are low priority. Yes to decisions related to your area which would negatively impact your team. And as a result, it's very easy to end up feeling quite disempowered with no sense of agency or control over your area.

This is a hangover from that 1980 authoritarian management style that should have been phased out just like the shoulder pads that went with it. You do still see individuals in organizations that have an authoritarian style and would be extremely challenged if you said no to them. But as a general rule, any decent manager or leader will be open to different opinions if they are presented in a constructive, positive and well-thought-through manner.

 How do I say no? See page 211.

Inspiring and impactful leaders are able to constructively challenge when they need to. They know how to influence upwards and sideways. And they're better able to negotiate their team's workload to persuade senior stakeholders to look again at decisions.

To be clear, I'm not talking about challenging someone's *authority*. I'm not talking about disrespecting the hierarchy at all. You can put forward a different viewpoint to a board member, a chief executive or a director without disrespecting either them or their authority as the ultimate decision maker. That is where those in Camp 2 often fall down. If someone believes that you don't respect their hierarchy, that you don't respect the decisions that they're making, or that you don't respect them as a person, then you are going to alienate them. This is problematic because it is almost impossible to influence someone that you have already alienated.

Decision-makers have responsibility for both the decisions and their consequences. They are often considering a number of different perspectives. And the more senior they are, the more likely it is that they can see the bigger picture because they have line of sight of more of the organization.

It's worth remembering that it's much easier to argue for a case from your perspective, and really believe you're right, than it is to see all of the perspectives and have ultimate responsibility for the decision. As a director of fundraising and marketing, I made decisions with absolute confidence that I was right most the time. When I moved into a chief executive role, I realized things really aren't that simple. I didn't always know what the right decision was, I didn't always have the data that I needed, and there were multiple perspectives to consider.

Here are six ways to constructively disagree with someone more senior than you:

1. Build your relationship with them

In Chapter 6 I shared my six-step model of influencing. Steps 1 and 2 are building a good relationship with the people you want to influence and understanding where they're coming from. If someone likes you, if you have built some form of rapport or connection, if they feel like you do actually like them and care about them as a person, then they will be more inclined to listen to you.

And if you have built a relationship with them, then you will have gathered some information about them, which will enable you to communicate in their language rather than in your language. And that's absolutely crucial for influencing.

2. Pick your battles

Don't disagree with everything – that's not constructive; it's just really annoying and if you're doing that then you're probably in the wrong organization. Equally, if you disagree with everything that your manager is doing, then it's time to take a step back and think about whether you want to work for this person or not. And if you do want to keep working for them, you'll need to reset your attitude toward them. Because if in your head you're thinking *"They're wrong and they don't know what they're doing"* they will pick up on that and it will be almost impossible to influence them and succeed in your role.

> *"I used to feel like I had to fight every battle for my team. Now I conserve my energy and think about whether it is a battle I can win and what the potential consequences of that are. I fight less battles and people seem to listen to me more now." Ella*

There may be some things that actually you feel quite strongly about, but you know that all the cards are stacked against you or that there is no way that someone's going to change their mind. In which case, put your point forward but don't make it a battle if you know that you cannot win.

3. Be solution-focused wherever possible

I am not encouraging you to complain. I am not encouraging you to just say a flat no to everything that your manager, your chief executive or your board members ask you to do. What I am encouraging you to do is to be confident in putting forward alternative solutions to solve problems and to be confident in reframing ways of looking at things.

I've got some useful phrases that you could use to do that. You could start by saying, *"What if we looked at this another way?"* and then explain your alternative viewpoint. You could ask, *"Can I offer an alternative perspective?"* Because you are asking it as a question, it's hard for someone to say, *"No, I don't want to hear your alternative perspective."*

Another question you could use is *"I have an alternative option I'd like to run past you, would you be open to hearing it?"* That softener question at the end demonstrates that you are respecting their authority.

4. Drop the "but"

If you start a response with *"but…"* you are signaling that you think they are wrong. Instead, try the phrase *"Yes, and…"* It acknowledges the value of their contribution, the other person will think you are building on what they are saying, and you'll be seen as constructive.

5. Speak truth to power when you really need to

There will be times when decisions being made really matter and have significant consequences for your ability to do your job well. Times where your expertise isn't being taken on board and you don't agree with the decision. You may know that you can't change the decision but you feel you need to speak up. This is often called speaking truth to power.

I have a great phrase that you can use in that situation – *"I wouldn't be doing my job properly if I didn't make sure you understood the potential consequences of that decision."* You are still respecting the fact that it is their decision to make. But you are making sure that they are making it from an informed basis, and that you have done your job in terms of reflecting the consequences.

I once had to tell a room full of board members at a global organization that they were making a very poor decision. I'd been brought in as an interim and my role included setting the fundraising strategy and targets for the next strategic period. As the organization was very hierarchical, all my communication had gone via the CEO until this meeting, so I had little opportunity to influence upwards. Instead of taking on board the stretching targets I'd developed with the team based on history, potential and our expertise, the board wanted to double the target.

And I used exactly that phrase. I asked to speak, I stood up and I said, *"I wouldn't be doing my job properly if I didn't make sure you understood the potential consequences of that decision."* And then elaborated on that. Because the consequences of that particular decision were huge.

The decision did go my way in the end. And I was really relieved about that. I would have felt like I hadn't done my job properly if I hadn't made them understand the flaws in their plan. I garnered a lot of respect from my colleagues because

I spoke truth to power in a way that people would listen to. It is something you do on occasion though, not regularly.

6. You don't need to apologize for having a different opinion

Often I will see people disagreeing with someone more senior than them and they'll start by saying *"I'm sorry, but..."* I don't think you need to apologize for having a different opinion. You've been hired for your expertise. You don't need to apologize for what you are saying; you just need to deliver it in a way that doesn't create tension and is seen as helping to move the conversation forward.

There are also some things that you can do long term when it comes to setting the boundaries and disagreeing with people more senior than you. If you are someone who is always saying yes to everything your manager throws at you and are feeling overwhelmed and overworked, then start by changing your automatic response in those situations. Instead of automatically responding with *"Yes,"* you could say, *"Let me think about how that sits with the existing priorities"* or *"Can I think through the practicalities of that and come back to you tomorrow?"*

You can start setting boundaries more clearly; for example, don't respond to emails that are sent at night. If your manager wants to send you an email at night, that's up to them but you don't have to respond. You don't have to be at the immediate beck and call of your manager at all times to be doing your job well. If you are being asked to take on work, and you genuinely don't think that you or your team can take on that workload, a sentence that I recommend is *"That sounds great. Where does it fit in with my existing priorities? Can we discuss that?"* Then you and the person handing the work to you are in agreement about where it fits.

You can also say, *"That's great. My team is at full capacity at the moment and working flat out. If we take that on, what would you suggest that we put on hold in order to be able to do that?"* Tone is really important with that phrase but the message is: we are not an endless resource.

I often see people at middle management level being treated as if they are an endless resource. All the work filters down to them. They say yes to it all, but they want to protect their team who are already overloaded. So it all just sits and piles up on them. And then they're either exhausted and overworked or they feel like they're failing because they've set themselves up for an impossible task.

It is a really useful skill to be able to push back to senior colleagues – to be able to say "this isn't a limitless resource." You also do need to be able to back that up. You need to be able to track or map in some way the fact that you're at capacity. If your manager does not trust or believe that you're all working hard, then it can be quite hard to have that discussion. So you need to be able to evidence what you're saying.

I know you may be reading this chapter and feeling uncomfortable about the idea of any form of potential conflict or difficult discussion. The advice I've shared will help you disagree without conflict and I also suggest using the Cloak of Authority tool.

Speaking the language of senior stakeholders

Not everybody thinks the same way as you do, so to communicate powerfully and influence it helps to be able to adapt your communication so that it lands with the listener.

Understand what matters to your audience

We all place value in different things. Some people value recognition and status, for example, while others value connection or the opportunity to contribute and make an impact. If you want to influence somebody, then it is helpful to know what they value. As anyone who has worked in sales knows, you have to position what you are offering as providing what they actually want.

When it comes to influencing stakeholders, it is helpful to think of yourself as a researcher and them as your research subject. Watch and listen to what they are telling you they value through their communication. If they are always talking about team and say "we" rather than "I" then you can use that same language when talking to them. If you notice that they are very proud of winning an award, then you know they value recognition and status and can build that into your proposal by giving them a leadership role.

The four questions people ask

When we are listening to a proposal, we fit that information into our model of the world based on our thinking preferences. We will be asking (either in our heads as we make sense of it or out loud) one or two of these four questions:

Why? Why does this matter – what is the purpose or context?

What? What exactly are we talking about? Sum it up for me.

How? How exactly will this work? Break it down for me step by step.

What if? What if X happens or Y doesn't happen? What will we do then?

Notice the questions that your senior stake-holders ask. This will allow you to tailor your communication to them and it will land much better as a result. This is such a simple but effective approach to take.

- A *Why* question might sound like "How does this fit with our strategic priorities?"
- A *What* question might be "What exactly do you need in terms of resources?"
- A *How* question might be "Do you have a detailed plan of action or timeline?"
- What if questions often involve raising different scenarios or asking "What if X happens? How are we factoring that in?"

Cover all four questions when presenting information. If you present without answering the question someone is asking, they won't be listening properly because they'll be thinking you have missed the most relevant point.

- If you don't give a *Why* person context, they will think you are focusing too much on detail and ignoring the bigger picture.
- If you don't summarize what *exactly* you are talking about, a *What* person will get lost.
- A *How* person needs to be able to picture how something will work in order to take it on board.
- A *What if* person can see potential issues and problems that others can't, but their questions can feel random and are not always welcomed.

"I've started using this approach when presenting and I've noticed my points are landing better now. It's so simple to remember too." Betty

Be intentional about your impact

Before any communication, it is useful to quickly thinking through **Feel/Think/Act**.

How do I want this person to **feel**?
What do I want this person to **think**?
What **action** do I want this person to take?

"I was presenting my new strategy to the board for approval and this was a really helpful structure to use. I wanted them to feel inspired, I wanted them to think it was well researched and I wanted them to get involved in its delivery. I tailored my communication accordingly and I got the feedback I was looking for." Sunita

Communicating with clarity to busy senior people

Senior stakeholders are often short on time and if you have an opportunity to present at a meeting with the board, you will likely have short timeslot. Make the most of it with these tips:

- Do your pre-work – you don't want to be going into a room unsure of what reaction you will receive. Have conversations individually beforehand where possible to understand the reception you will get and have some advocates in the room.
- Be concise – you can provide more detail if asked.
- Summarize the conclusion and implications at the start rather than ending with them – they don't need to hear the whole story of how you came to these conclusions.
- Include any major assumptions you have made.
- If you present multiple options and have a prefer- ence, then share that preference and explain why.
- Take the supporting information with you so that you have it to hand.
- Frame your proposal as solving organizational prob- lems that they care about so they see its relevance.

Handling objections and difficult questions

If you can reframe how you view objections and difficult questions, it will take your influencing and leadership skills to a whole new level. If you see influencing as something you do *to* others then it can feel like an objection or difficult question threatens to send you off course. But if you see influencing as something you do *with* others, all objections and questions are useful information which enrich the conversation.

> *"I realized that I had to stop taking objections so personally. I would feel attacked in board meetings when colleagues raised challenging questions and then I was on the back foot for the rest of the meeting. Now I can see that people are asking questions because they need more information, or they need it presented in a way that makes more sense to them." Dee*

We all think differently and place emphasis on different things, so the fact that questions are being asked doesn't mean you've failed in your communication. It's actually brilliant that colleagues are raising these questions because they are engaging, they are telling you what concerns they have about it, and helping you to look at the proposal from a variety of angles to make it even stronger.

And they are telling you what is important to them, which is information you can use to help them understand the benefits of what you are proposing. If you can be the person who welcomes all feedback and questions, using it to improve your proposal and build support for it, then you are truly leading and showing the growth mindset we talked about earlier.

So how do you respond to challenging questions?

If you notice you are triggered, take a moment to breathe so you can respond rather than react. Then get the questioner on side with a holding phrase like *"That's a great question..."*

The key to a powerful response is to think about what is driving their question and respond to that or explore it further, while also answering the question they asked. Here's what that might look like in practice:

Stakeholder: *"How long will this project take?"*

Your old answer: *"Three months."*

Answer that speaks to their underlying concern: *"We'll work the timing so it doesn't compete with project X and it should take three months in total."*

Answer that explores their possible concerns: *"Three months – does that bring up any resource or timing issues for your team that we need to work around?"*

Finally, you may need to keep the conversation on track. If someone is using the discussion to further their own agenda at the cost of yours, you may need to rein it back in and request everyone stays focused on the topic at hand. Or if someone is being overtly negative without adding any value to the discussion, you could ask them to be specific about their concerns.

Chapter 7: Top tips

- Think of you and your manager as partners on the same team and see part of your role as helping them to succeed.

- Be clear on what you need from your manager and ask for it.

- You can challenge a decision without challenging someone's authority but pick your battles.

- Make sure you cover the four questions people ask when communicating to senior stakeholders – Why? What? How? What if?

- Think about how you want someone to Feel, Think and Act when communicating to them.

- See objections and difficult questions as providing valuable information rather than a judgment about your abilities.

Part 4

Taking control of your career

Now that you're seeing yourself as a leader, you're being seen by others as a leader and you've been taking steps to increase your influence and impact, it is time to focus on developing your career. Closing the Influence Gap means being recognized for your contribution and your potential so we'll be looking at how you can take control of your career and the secrets to succeeding at each new level of leadership.

Given you are reading this book, I hope I'm preaching to the choir here but I'm going to say it anyway. You can't leave your career prospects and development in the hands of your line manager and hope that they recognize your potential. They have many other things on their mind and their priorities may not align with yours. A 2018 survey by Deloitte showed that 58% of people rated their employer as not effective or only somewhat effective at empowering people to manage their own careers.[1] These chapters will support you as you take steps to manage your own career.

Chapter 8 – Preparing for promotion

Whether you're looking to stay with your current employer or secure a new job elsewhere, there are steps you can take to prepare for that move, from improving your interview skills to becoming more visible.

Chapter 9 – Succeeding in your new role

Each new level of leadership brings its own unique challenges and it helps to be prepared for those and to start your new role the way you mean to go on.

Chapter 8

Preparing for promotion

I encourage women to have career conversations with their managers so that their managers can advocate for them. We'll talk about visibility later in this chapter, but as a foundational step I'd encourage you to ask your manager to support your career aspirations and be specific in your requests for opportunities, training and visibility.

In this chapter we are going to cover how you can assess your skills and identify areas for development. Then we'll look at what you can do to prepare to move up to the next level. Finally, we'll explore how you can become more visible so that decision makers can see the value you bring to your organization.

 ## Coaching tool: The Leadership Wheel

In order to develop your career, it helps if you can accurately assess your performance in your current role, know your strengths, and recognize and work on your areas for development. This simple tool will help you to do exactly that.

You can also apply it to the job you want to have, using it to map out the skills or experience you need to gain to be a credible candidate at that next level up.

Within the online resources at www.carlamillertraining.com/bookresources you'll find a blank template of a Leadership Wheel. Here's how to use it:

1. Spend some time listing the different areas of your role (or the role you want to have) that you need to be good at. These might be technical skills, leadership skills or more general skills such as presenting or networking. Write down any that come to mind and review your annual objectives for further inspiration. If you're using this to map out your path to your next role, then base your list on the role you want, not the one you currently have.

2. Identify the eight skills or areas from your list which you really need to excel at to succeed. These are likely to be a mix of things you are already good at and those where you have room for improvement.

3. Allocate one segment of the Leadership Wheel to each of those eight areas and then score yourself out of 10 for each segment and use a cross to represent that on the wheel. If you know that you are naturally self-critical, then turn into your Inner Leader beforehand and calibrate your scoring by discussing it with your line manager or a colleague whose opinion you value. Here's an example of a completed wheel for you.

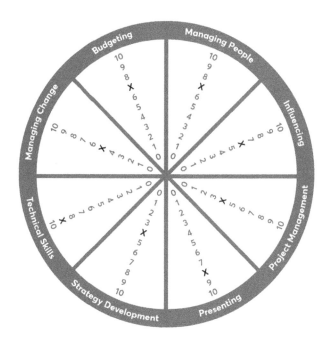

4. Realistically, we are not aiming for 10/10 on every-thing. Whatever your score, recognize that you are already doing your job well and congratulate yourself for the areas where you are scoring highly. If you are new to your role (or aspiring to the next role), know that this is a journey and that wherever you are is okay.

5. Pick an area that you want to work on this month and ask yourself, *"What steps could I take this month increase my score by one point?"*. Then commit to that action and go and take the first step straight away.

In the example wheel, the person has rated themselves as 4 out of 10 for strategy development, for example, so they might decide to grab a book on strategy one month so they feel confident they know the basics. The next month they might ask to contribute to a strategy discussion or talk to a leader, learning from them about how to create strategies collaboratively.

> *"I came to coaching with this vague feeling that I wasn't good enough at my job. The Leadership Wheel tool helped me accurately assess my skills and make an action plan. Plus I was able to recognize that actually I'm performing well in my job."* Sabeena

If you've put confidence, communication, networking or influencing on your wheel as areas for development, check out the Influence & Impact course or my podcast to help move you up lots of points.

Preparing to step up to the next level

There are some signs to look out for which indicate that you are ready to step up to the next level and apply for a promotion or a job elsewhere:

- Getting bored because you're missing learning and new challenges.
- Seeing how things could be improved but not having the authority to create change yourself.
- Thinking organizationally rather than just about your team.
- Others suggesting it.
- Wanting to step out of your comfort zone.

■ Being asked to stand in for your manager frequently
or being given additional responsibilities beyond your
job title.

If you are someone who gets frustrated by the slow progress in your organization, it could be a sign that you are not
yet operating at the level which will make best use of your
natural strengths. I am a natural change maker and I got
very frustrated in more junior roles because I couldn't make
any changes to improve things. It was only when I became
a director that I really found the level where I excelled and
could use those skills effectively. So if that is you too, don't
give up hope!

You may not *feel* ready. But it's important to check in with
yourself and see how much of that doubt comes from your
Inner Critic or imposter feelings. If, alongside any worries,
you are feeling excited by the potential of the next level and
pulled toward it, then check in with your Inner Leader to tune
in to your intuition without fear clouding your judgment.

Perhaps you doubt your ability to lead? I often coach
women who worry that they are not natural leaders. This
comes up a lot with women who are naturally introverted
or are more task orientated than people orientated. These
women look at how others lead and find themselves lacking
in comparison. I am quick to reassure them that there is no
perfect personality profile for brilliant leaders. There are
many different and equally effective ways to lead and leadership skills can be developed. In fact, we should all be learning
leaders. If this resonates with you, check out the Personal

Leadership Brand coaching tool in Chapter 4, which will help you to own all that you bring to leadership.

You may be ready for more but not the job that your employer is suggesting you apply for. Just because your manager is leaving and you are capable of doing their job, it doesn't mean that you want to do it. If you've always looked at their job and thought it would be a nightmare then it probably would be a nightmare. You're not obliged to apply for a promotion just because someone else wants you to. Many people are content at their current level or embrace a more "squiggly" career, where they follow passions and interests rather than climbing a ladder of seniority.[1]

Alternatively, others may not believe you are ready. It is always a good idea to talk to your manager about your aspirations so they can help you to achieve them and build up the skills and experience you need. If your manager isn't supportive, you may be able to find someone else who can mentor and support you in that way.

Your manager may not think you are ready – in which case listen to their feedback but decide for yourself how valid their points are. They may not be able to offer you opportunities in your current organization but as an external candidate in a different organization you will be seen differently. I had a manager who told me I was trying to run before I could walk and very actively discouraged me from applying for an internal promotion. I knew I could do more and secured a role at the next level elsewhere very easily because they could see my potential.

There are some practical steps you can take now which will get you ready to move up to the next level successfully.

- **Look at the job descriptions of the roles that interest you** and see what skills and experience you need. Then take action to gain those skills and experience or demonstrate those attributes, whether in a work or voluntary capacity. There are many good causes needing trustees, which can be an excellent way to evidence your leadership ability.
- **Have coffee with a few people who are already doing those roles** to find out what the role is like in reality and what they wish they'd known before they started.
- **Start telling people about the roles you are interested in** so they can keep an eye on for opportunities for you.
- **Talk to recruitment consultants** to get their input on whether your CV is a good fit for the role and how you can improve it.

What got you here won't get you there

Each new level of leadership brings its own unique challenges and requires a different mindset. The things that make you successful at your current level won't all map across to success at the next level. The important thing is to recognize that and quickly map out what it takes to thrive at your new level. This book will help with that and for inspiration you can also look at people you admire at that level and see how they approach things. I also suggest building a network of peers; one of the reasons my Influence & Impact course is so powerful is the peer support that the women offer each other which makes them feel less alone.

If you're moving into your first management role, for example, then you'll be used to doing everything yourself, while succeeding as a new manager will be about learning how to deliver through a team and empower others. The delegation section in Chapter 4 will prove useful for you.

"It was so hard to stop doing everything myself but I've learnt to trust my team with my reputation, which was terrifying at first. My role is to support and guide them to deliver at a high level." Katy

If you're moving to a head of team role, you may find yourself managing people who know more than you, which requires a different approach. We'll explore this transition from specialist to generalist in Chapter 9.

If you are taking on your first director role, you'll need to be able to think beyond advocating for your team and start thinking more organizationally. There will be times when as part of being a director you'll make decisions which are best for the organization but come at a cost to your department.

"This was a huge mindset shift for me as a new director to move from advocating for my team to being able to look at the bigger picture. At first, I felt guilty but I learnt to make my case well and then put that aside to engage in the discussion with an open mind." Renee

And if it is a CEO role you'd like to step up to, you'll be adjusting to the new level of responsibility and the fact that you could find yourself making important decisions without knowing what the right solution is. Not to mention managing yourself as you won't have the feedback and support of a manager (or if you work for a charity you could find yourself with multiple bosses in the form of trustees).

There are two skills which will help you whatever level you wish to move up to. The first is emotional intelligence and in particular self-awareness. Understanding yourself and the impact you have on others will make you a much better leader, which is why as a leader personal development is as valuable as professional development. My hope is that this book will support you in that.

The second is influencing skills because the more senior you become, the more time you will spend navigating internally. Your success will be dependent on your ability to build relationships with peers, overcome tensions and influence senior stakeholders, both internal and external.

Succeeding at interview

Once you've done your preparation to move to a new role then you've got to secure it! If you'd like to find interviews less anxiety-producing and perform better, this is the chapter for you.

I spent a couple of years recruiting to senior roles in the charity sector and running a recruitment business, so I've included some of my top tips for you here. If you'd like to dive deeper on this, I also have an audio course called Instant Interview Confidence, which shares my seven steps to success at management and leadership interviews.[2]

Preparing for your interview

You want to be prepared for your interview, but overpreparing can be unhelpful – you've packed your brain with so much information that it could be hard to find the most relevant information when you need it in an interview.

What I do suggest doing is going through the job description and noting next to each of the points an example you could use if they ask you about it. You won't use 90% of those examples but this prep work will mean they are front of mind and you won't have that blank moment where your brain is searching for an example out of nowhere. Do a quick run-through of how you would tell the story so that you are portraying yourself in the best light.

If you are someone who struggles to judge how much to share in an answer and are too concise or too verbose, this structure could help:

- **Situation** (describe the scenario succinctly)
- **Goal** (what were you aiming to do?)
- **Strategy** (what approach did you take and why?)
- **Outcome** (what was the end result?)
- **Lessons** (what if anything did you learn?)

Remember, interviewers don't really care about anything other than your way of thinking and interacting with people, so they really don't want detail that isn't highly relevant. If you don't have one perfect example then draw on your real-life experiences and merge a couple of scenarios into one. As long as it is a real representation of how you have acted in a similar scenario, you are still answering with integrity while showing them what you are capable of. We are aiming for them to be able to picture you doing the role.

Be sure to have example of when you've had to deal with challenging situations with a team member, a peer and managing upwards, as these areas often come up in interviews at a senior level. You'll also want to be able talk about your management or leadership style and how a manager can bring out the best out in you.

Do your general research on the organization including their social media activity and in particular the area of the organization you'll be working in. You can then drop some of these into your answers to show that you have done your homework.

And yes, informal interviews still require prep – they may feel relaxed in tone but they are still part of the process of sifting through candidates.

Feeling and appearing confident at interview

You've now got some very useful tools for this:

- Tune in to your Inner Leader before the interview so that when you start the interview you are feeling calm, confident and grounded.
- Visualize leaving your Inner Critic outside the building (or outside your front door if you're having a virtual interview).
- Use some of the tips in your Meeting Toolkit around starting and ending strong so that you appear confident in the way you present yourself.

My favorite interview technique is to think about how you would want the interviewers to describe you when they discuss you afterwards. As I shared in Chapter 4 on your Personal Leadership Brand, being intentional about this will help you to filter the language you use. If in doubt go for *"She wants the job, she'd be great at the job and she'd be great to work with."*

> *"I went into the interview wanting to be seen as strategic as I've had feedback in the past that I didn't come across as a strategic thinker. I drew on examples of creating strategies and also strategic decision making. After the interview, the recruiter shared that I'd been described as someone who would bring strategic thinking to the team."* Mel

It is also worth reframing how you think about interviews if you get nervous about them. Interviews are not a judgment of your abilities – they are a discussion which enables both the interviewers and the interviewees to see if this is a good fit. Both parties have the right to decide it isn't a good fit or to keep the discussion going at another interview. If you don't get the job, you are not being rejected – they just found someone they thought would be a better fit or they can't picture you in the role.

Blow your own trumpet

It can be hard for many women to celebrate their own achievements and own their expertise. In interviews it is not only socially acceptable to blow your own trumpet (translation for non-Brits: talk about how great you are) – it is *necessary*. The interviewers are *asking* you to tell them about your experience, skills, expertise and attributes. So give yourself permission to own your awesomeness. Trust me, if you struggle with this then there is zero chance of you being seen as arrogant.

While it is great to be the sort of leader that says "we" more than you say "I", they are not interviewing your team – they are interviewing you. When you talk about an achievement, they specifically want to know about your contribution to it. So drastically reduce your use of *"we"* in interviews and say *"I"* a lot more.

The psychology of interviews

Interviews are essentially a bit of a game; as well as show-casing your skills, experience and attributes, you also need to show that you understand that game. When you are applying for most roles, the balance of power sits entirely in favor of the interview panel right up until they offer you the role, when it flips over to you. The more senior you are, the more equal the balance of power is from the beginning and at CEO level it should feel like a genuinely two-way process.

Your role is not to judge interviewers' questions, but to work out what they are really asking and how you can provide them with an answer that has integrity and tells them what they need to know. If you are someone who sits in interviews bemused by why they've asked such a stupid question, they will read that on your face, so try and think *"there's no such thing as a stupid question."*

Hopefully, the days of totally inappropriate questions at interview are behind us, but as I write this the world of recruitment has finally caught on to the fact that asking for your current salary just exacerbates the existing gender pay gap. The average female executive earns £423,000 less over the lifetime of her career than her male counterpart.[3] The gender pay gap starts in our starting roles and then widens from there. This gap is even wider for women of color. Employers should be paying a fair salary for the role and select the best person, not judge your financial value based on what your current employer pays you.

If you are asked for your current salary you can say:

- "Given my experience and skills, I'm looking for a salary in the range of x to x."
- "I'm keen to understand the salary you've budgeted for this role."
- "I prefer to focus on the value that I can add to this position, rather than what I'm paid in my current role."

Have some questions up your sleeve for the end of the interview that focus on the things that are important to you, such as development opportunities or organizational culture, and also demonstrate that you've done your homework. Save your really challenging questions for once you've secured the job offer. At that point, you can also ask for more information, which is a chance to chat to the team or peers or whatever you need to know that this is the right move for you.

If I've enjoyed the interview and I want the job, I like to end the interview with two final points. First I ask if they have any concerns about my ability to do the role well. This gives me a chance to understand and address those concerns directly. Then I say I've really enjoyed meeting them and

I am definitely interested in the role and look forward to hearing from them.

After the interview

It never does any harm to reach out and thank the interviewers, saying it was nice to meet them; LinkedIn or email is a good way to do that. Keep it short though – don't be tempted to add to your interview answers or ask for more information.

Tune in to your Inner Leader again as your Inner Critic will want to beat you up about any answers that weren't perfect or get busy imagining worst-case scenarios. I like to trust that if it is meant to be, it is meant to be.

If they offer you the job, it is acceptable to ask for time to sleep on it to make sure it is the right decision for you. Often we are so focused on jumping through hoops to get the job that we haven't tuned in to our intuition to see if we actually want the job. It is reasonable to ask for 24 or 48 hours to consider the offer – be sure to be very positive about it and say you're excited but are someone who likes to reflect on big life decisions. They may not like it – at that point they just want you to say yes and may have other candidates as back-up options, but as long as you are not stringing them along while waiting for another offer to come through then it is a fair request if you'd like time to reflect.

You may also want to negotiate on salary, particularly if there is a salary range. I have always asked for the top of the range on the logic that I was the best person for the job since they'd given it to me. This is easier to negotiate through a recruiter but you can always make the following point: *"Thank you for this offer and I'm really excited about this role. Is there any leeway on salary negation as I was hoping for the top of the range and I believe that is the market value for my skills."*

If they say no, then you could request a salary review built into your six-month performance review and/or agree annual salary reviews. You can couch this in terms of *"I want to stay here long term so I don't want to be stuck on the same salary when I have more experience under my belt."* I also think there is room to negotiate if you are working a four-day week but doing a five-day job with all the responsibilities; I would try and meet in the middle between the pro rata salary and the full salary. Ultimately, you have to read the room in these discussions to judge how open they are to negotiation; do your research on your market value and determine how important salary is to you.

Being more visible

A final piece of preparing for promotion is to demonstrate your strengths and successes to others and get yourself on the radar of key stakeholders. Just the thought of that makes many of us feel uncomfortable. It goes against so many of the (subliminal and not so subliminal) messages society sends us about how women should be modest and not draw attention to ourselves – yes, the struggle against the patriarchy is indeed a real one!

To close the Influence Gap we need to be seen and heard. I've shared a lot of strategies for getting your voice heard but how about being more visible and getting noticed?

Feeling safe to be seen

At some level many of us fear being criticized if we draw attention to ourselves. If that resonates with you then you can run that belief through the reframing beliefs exercise in Chapter 2 and reframe it into something more helpful. If being visible feels like a fundamentally unsafe thing to do, that may be a response to past trauma and working through it with a therapist could be helpful.

Trying to avoid judgment by staying small is an Inner Critic strategy and it won't allow you to fulfill your potential. Most of us are way too busy thinking about ourselves to spare more than a passing thought about other people. Try and focus on what you think about yourself, not the opinions of others, or you're giving away all your power to someone else to determine if you are good enough.

The myth of meritocracy

In her enlightening book, *Why Men Win at Work*, former VP at Proctor & Gamble, Gill Whitty-Collins, talks about how women believe in the "myth of meritocracy" – that when we work hard and do a good job we will be recognized and rewarded for it. By contrast, she says "Men are more comfortable self-marketing away, so their work is much more visible to their managers and much more likely to be recognized and rewarded (with a bigger salary, a better job, a promotion)."[4] That really rang true for me. I'm sure I'm not alone in noticing that while women tend to be brilliant at bigging up their team and often use the term "we", men will more often use the word "I" when talking about successes.

You can take small steps toward becoming more visible like those listed here. No need to grab the microphone and shout "I'm ready to be seen."

Top tips for visibility

- When you've done the work and not your team, own that by saying "I" instead of defaulting to "we" by habit.

- Articulate the problems you've been solving for the organization rather than just sharing the end result – you need to show people that you've been working hard and dealing with challenges.

- Spend an extra minute or two at the end of a meeting chatting to someone more senior than you.

- Share a relevant article or podcast episode you found useful with an audience wider than your close circle of colleagues.

- Suggest ideas or solutions at an all-company meeting or ask a positive and intelligent question.

- Tell someone senior to you what you admire about them and ask their advice on how you can hone that skill too.

- Share your longer-term goals in conversation – *"I have a long-term goal to become a CEO."*

- Ask for opportunities to work directly with senior stakeholders or key clients.

- Ask an inspiring leader to be your sponsor and tell them what you'd like to achieve through that.

- Give a lunchtime talk for colleagues or write a blog post for the intranet.

- Write a LinkedIn article on your area of expertise.

- Ask to be in the room at the level above you for key meetings and be clear on the value you could add.

- Put yourself forward for new opportunities like working groups or public relations opportunities.

- Share your team's successes widely and own the part you played in that too.

- If you struggle when talking about your abilities, you don't need to go to the other extreme and then worry about sounding arrogant. Try and be just 10% bolder when claiming your strengths. No-one is going to judge you for saying *"I'm good at that"* – you are not claiming to be the best at it.

Chapter 9

Succeeding in your new role

So you've successfully secured your new role – how do you start as you mean to go on? That's what we are going to cover in this chapter, alongside how to handle the shift from specialist manager to generalist leader and what to do if you've been promoted above your peers.

Starting a new job well

Follow these tips and you'll start your new role feeling confident.

1. Be intentional about your first impressions

A new role is a fantastic opportunity to be intentional about how you want to be perceived by others. How do you want your team, your new manager, your peers and your new CEO to experience and describe you? This is a great opportunity to use the Personal Leadership Brand coaching tool from Chapter 4.

2. Identify your key internal stakeholders

These are the people who are going to have an impact on your ability to deliver in your role or make decisions that impact your team. The more senior you are, the more important this is, so review Chapter 6 on navigating internal politics to learn about strategic relationship building.

3. Get clarity on your objectives

Make sure that you have a discussion with your line manager about your objectives for the first one, three and six months so that you share the same understanding of what good performance looks like. Often line managers let this slip, but you really want to know what success looks like or you could be working incredibly hard but focusing your effort in the wrong areas. I had a client who thought she was doing well in her new role until her three-month review, when it turned out she had different priorities from her line manager and they weren't happy with her performance. We worked together to rebuild her confidence and also get clarity on her objectives and priorities.

While you're having the discussion with your line manager, go beyond tasks and talk about the behaviors that they expect to see from a leader at this level. Ask what good leadership looks like within the organization and to them. There may be organizational behaviors that give you a clear steer, but each line manager has different expectations and communication preferences.

4. Check the appetite for change

In leadership roles it is vital that you and your employer are on the same page when it comes to the appetite for change. Interviews are often not a great indication of this. As a recruiter, I saw many new leaders struggle because their desire to make change was not matched by their employer's desire. If you think you have a remit to shake things up, get clarity on what exactly you can shake up; if it is linked to culture change, assess how willing senior leadership are to change their own behavior. If you're providing cover for parental leave, be sure to get on the same page as the person you are covering for before they head off.

5. Create your 90-day plan

After getting clear on your objectives (or prompting that discussion if your manager isn't taking the initiative), you can turn this into a 90-day plan that outlines what you are aiming to achieve in your first 30, 60 and 90 days. Much of this will be about observing and connecting in the first 30 days in particular. This is a great document to share with your team, who will be wondering what your plans are for implementing any changes and trying to establish if you are a friend or foe. It can be reassuring to say to your team: *"I'm going to spend my first 30 days observing, understanding the detail of how things work and asking a lot of questions. I have plenty of ideas but I really want to know how things work here first and get your input."*

6. Map the dynamics

Often we have a desire to quickly prove ourselves in a new role, but you don't have to spring into action straight away. Take time to listen to your team and observe how they perform and relate to each other and other teams. Watch your manager in action and observe their communication style, priorities and leadership style. Notice what gets celebrated by the senior leaders and CEO and the dynamics of the group if you're sat at the table as a director.

You're doing this for two reasons. First to understand the organization and its people better so that you can work in a way that aligns with others rather than imposing your strategies on them – it will improve the quality of your thinking. The second reason is for influencing – when you have this information, you will be better placed to implement your influencing strategy and speak the language of your stakeholders.

7. Keep an eye out for the Valley of Doom

When I was having an overwhelmed moment in my first director role, someone told me about the Valley of Doom; it made me feel better so I'm sharing it with you. When you start a new job you are full of hope. You can see all the potential in the role and the organization and you have rose-tinted glasses on so you assume that there will be none of the flaws of your previous organization (and you'll have magically left your flaws behind too).

And it all goes along swimmingly until something happens that makes you take off your rose-tinted glasses. At the time I kept asking questions and wishing I hadn't when I heard the answers. It was my role to solve problems, which were much more numerous than I had expected at a team and organizational level. At director level these are often issues that aren't discussed at interview because they involve the very people interviewing you!

At that point you fall off the edge of the cliff into the Valley of Doom. When you're in the Valley of Doom everything goes from looking possible to looking impossible and the disappointment is real. But actually, it is just the reality of the fact that no organization is perfect and this organization has fallen off the pedestal you placed it on.

Your time in the Valley of Doom won't last long; you just have to ride it out. It may be very tempting to think it is too hard and to quit. But as you start to build relationships and see that you can make a positive difference, you will come out of it as quickly as you fell in. You'll be positive again, but this time it will be realistic optimism rather than blind optimism. So if you are experiencing that Valley of Doom feeling, rest assured that it won't last forever.

Moving from specialist to generalist

As you develop your career and become more senior, there's a good chance that you'll move from being a specialist to a generalist. It is helpful to approach that with the right mindset as it can be hard to navigate that shift.

In a typical office environment, many people start off in a generalist role as an assistant or coordinator, helping the team with anything and everything. As you progress you become more specialized in a particular area and when you reach management or head of level, you're an expert in that area. But as you become even more senior you will eventually find yourself managing people with different specialisms who know more about their areas of work than you do.

Here are seven strategies to help you succeed when you step up into a generalist role.

1. Start with mutual respect

Come from a place of mutual respect and trust with your direct reports. Start with the assumption that you are all really good at your jobs. This builds instant trust and means you don't need to prove yourself by trying to know absolutely everything straight away. Don't fake it 'til you make it. You'll build more credibility by being transparent about what you do and don't know.

2. Be great at asking questions

You don't need to have all the answers, make every decision or solve all of the problems. Thinking that you do will send any imposter feelings into overdrive. In fact, as you move into a generalist position, this won't always be possible and it will drive your direct reports crazy. Make it your focus to get great at asking questions.

> *"I was really struggling with imposter feelings when I started managing people who had more experience in their area than I did. I felt this pressure to prove that I deserved to be there by having all the right answers. It was such a relief to realize I didn't need to know more than them to be able to be a good leader and support them."* Sharon

3. Take a coaching approach

Adopt a coaching style of leadership where you ask lots of questions and support them to find their own answers. There are some great articles on how to do this if you search online, as well as courses on coaching skills for managers. Coaching is a powerful way of helping others to think about situations or challenges differently and I think all leaders benefit from having coaching skills.

4. Set boundaries

Just because the people you manage know more about their area than you do, it doesn't mean they can do what they want with no accountability!

Make it clear that you will be held responsible for everything they do and that you need to understand it so that you can support them where needed. This isn't about micromanaging or trying to know as much about their specialism as they do. You can agree with each person what you need to know, how often you need an update and in what format.

5. Have clear objectives and KPIs

Co-create KPIs with the people you're managing. You want to be able to check in and see that they're making progress. If they're not achieving these, then you need to be able to problem solve with them to identify what the issue is and what support they need.

Without objectives or KPIs, you won't be able to keep them accountable or step in to support them when needed.

6. Advocate for them

You will need to navigate internally to get your team resources, influence on their behalf, get decisions made and ensure they get the profile and recognition they deserve. Have a conversation and ask them what they need from you in terms of advocacy and influence. Don't forget to feedback when you are championing them. You might be advocating for your team in meetings but if they're unaware they can feel unsupported.

7. Be aware of your biases

Be conscious of your biases toward different areas, specialisms or ways of working. This is particularly important if you're still managing your own specialism as well. It can be incredibly demotivating to have a manager who doesn't take an interest in your area or favors others over you.

Take an active interest in and responsibility for all areas you're managing and make an effort. Ask the specialists you're managing some of the key things you need to know and learn them – you might even like to do a short course on it!

Adapting after being promoted above your peers

I am asked about this scenario often so I wanted to dive deep on how you navigate the transition from friend and peer to manager. You'll also want to explore Part 2, which is all about being seen as a leader.

The emotional fallout

Leadership is a delicate balance at the best of times, but no more so than when you've been promoted above your peers, which can be a difficult transition to manage.

You might be thinking:

"Yes, my line manager thinks I can do this but do my colleagues believe I can do this job?"
"How is this going to impact my relationship with my friend who was my peer until now?"
"How am I going to manage that person I always clash with?"
"Is X going to be really annoyed I got the job and they didn't?"
"Can I really do this?"
"What if they made a mistake giving me the role?"

Those are all normal reactions to this situation. Imposter feelings and your Inner Critic are bound to crop up because you've stepped right outside of your comfort zone. I also see clients experiencing guilt if they were successful in being promoted and work friends or peers were unsuccessful. If that is you then it may help to remember that you are not the person who made the decision and it is not your responsibility.

You may also be fearing judgment by your new direct reports. It's important to remember that you can't actually mind read so you have no idea what they think about your ability to do the role. They may well have an opinion on your appointment but that can change once you get going – I have had to win over many reluctant direct reports in the past and they often became good friends.

You are probably not going to be perfect at your new job from day one – no-one would be – but you can adopt a growth mindset and commit to improving and becoming better at your job each day. I find that when imposter feelings kick in, it helps to focus on serving other people instead of worrying what they think of me.

Your first conversations with your new team members

Your new direct reports may be totally fine about your promotion or they may have some strong feelings about the situation.

If they applied for the role and didn't get it, they may be feeling undervalued or hard done by. If a structure has changed and they are now reporting to you instead of someone more senior, they may feel like they've effectively been demoted. There could be all sorts of different things going on within their heads so I recommend some honest one-to-one conversations with them about it. Some good questions to ask include:

> *"How can I best support you?"*
> *"Is there anything you are worried about?"*
> *"What makes you feel valued?"*
> *"What do you need from me?"*

Then the two of you can agree a way of working together and problem solve any issues together. You can agree how often you'll meet, what level of information you need and how often you need it. You can go through their objectives together and talk through any areas where you can support them and also talk about their wider career and development goals.

You may have mismatched expectations. There is usually at least one person who says they are totally self-sufficient and won't need your input at all. With those people you'll need to have the conversation which explains that you are responsible for their area and will therefore need oversight and input, but you can discuss together where you can add most value. Let them know you want to make their job easier, not harder, and if you can trust each other that will set a solid foundation. You can use the Cloak of Authority tool to help you with these conversations.

If you have good relationships with some people you work with, and not so good with others, you will have a bias. You'll naturally want to give the people you like the benefit of the doubt, while you won't be doing that for people you like less. So you have to be very conscious of that potential for bias and rebalance it.

> *"I started managing one of my friends and it took a bit of adjustment. We agreed that conversations about work belong and stay at work. The other team members need to be able to trust that what they share with me remains confidential. Things have changed in our friendship – I feel I can't moan about the leadership team anymore and sometimes that is awkward but we've made it work."* Jennie

Adapting your leadership style

Notice the communication styles that your team members prefer and adapt your communication accordingly. Also become aware of and celebrate their strengths so that they feel seen and valued.

It is definitely harder to establish your authority and leadership brand when you've previously held more junior roles in the organization. But there are some benefits in that you already have some existing relationships and knowledge of the organization, which means you can hit the ground running. You can use the Personal Leadership Brand tool in Chapter 4 to help you decide what sort of leader you want to be and how you want to be perceived by others.

As a team you can co-create your culture together. You can have a meeting or away day and talk about how often you want to meet and the format, how you can tackle the things that stop you doing your jobs well and how you want to work together.

Find a new support network

You won't be able to share everything with your former peers unedited anymore – it's just not appropriate. I encourage you to find yourself a new group of peers and get to know other people in your organization that are operating at this level. It will help to have them as sounding boards and friends and will also make influencing and dealing with tension between departments a lot easier.

Top tips

- Do more listening than talking.

- Focus on asking questions more than always providing answers.

- Make sure you have clarity on what it looks like to do your job really well so you and your manager are on the same page.

- Make a 90-day plan.

- Adapt your leadership style to suit the person and situation.

Part 5

Troubleshooting Q&A

When I coach women, either individually or within my Influence & Impact course, I create a safe space and they will
often raise questions that they can't ask elsewhere. Some of
these questions may have come up for you too so I wanted to
share them within this book.

How do I recover from a bullying boss?

"My former manager really knocked my confidence. It felt like I couldn't do anything right. I'm in a new job now and my new manager is lovely but I am still full of self-doubt and finding it hard to believe in myself again."

Those ghosts of bullying bosses can haunt us for a long time. They can leave us full of self-doubt in our next role and make us super-sensitive, so we start seeing criticism and negative feedback in every statement our new boss makes.

Let's start by understanding why negative feedback is the unwanted gift that just keeps on giving. We are actually psychologically programmed to remember negative feedback more.[1]

When someone gives us praise or positive feedback, we get a fleeting moment of happy emotion and then quickly forget about it. But when someone gives us negative feedback, it plays into something known as negativity bias. We pay more attention to the bad things that happen, we think about them more when they happen and make them seem more important than they actually are. Those memories get stored in the part of our brain where we store our thoughts and so we recall them word for word. And every time we replay those words in our heads, they recreate the negative feelings associated with them.

One of the other reasons we remember negative feedback more is because it feeds into some of the fears that we have about not being good enough. It seems to be part of the human experience that, at some level, all of us fear that we're not good enough.

So when somebody gives you some negative feedback, it fuels that fear.

"Maybe that means I'm not good enough."

"Maybe I wasn't cut out for this."

"What was I even thinking, to imagine that I could do this?"

If you are feeling like your confidence has been knocked, please don't beat yourself up for it. You are just being human. Very, very beautifully human. I've had my own experience of bullying bosses that led to so much stress it made me physically ill and made me doubt whether I could ever have a job I enjoyed.

What most people do when they've had a bullying boss is to just try and bury the experience deep down where they never have to think about it again. The methods I'm going to share with you will help you to leave the past behind you.

Step 1 – Recognize it is their voice that you're hearing, not yours

Start to notice when and how the self-doubt crops up that reminds you of a bullying boss. You might recognize a phrase that they used. It could be there was a particular personality trait or area of your work where they were very critical. Or you may notice it through how your body reacts, perhaps your shoulders get really tense, or you find your jaw is tensing. That's how you know that it is their voice in your head and not yours.

The reason that you want to be able to recognize it is to create some separation from the rest of your thoughts. You don't want to be carrying around somebody else's thoughts, opinions and judgments about us. So when you recognize it's their voice, name it as theirs.

Let's say your ex-boss is called Gertrude. When you recognize her impact on you, you say to yourself *"Oh that's Gertrude speaking. That's not me speaking."* Then you can choose – *"do I actually want to listen to Gertrude?"* You can choose not to listen if you don't want to. Simply noticing when their voice is coming up in your head can be really helpful.

Step 2 – Quieten their voice

Much like we do with the Inner Critic, there are some fun ways to use your imagination to take this version of Gertrude you're carrying around with you a lot less seriously. When she is being vocal, you can imagine her getting smaller and smaller and smaller and smaller until she's really tiny and laughable instead of being this scary presence in your mind. Or you can imagine her voice getting more and more high pitched until it's quite ridiculous. Or placing her in a small box and locking it. It sounds silly, but this simple exercise can be remarkably effective.

Step 3 – Create your feedback folder

Start creating a collection of great feedback that you get in an email folder or on your phone or a Word document. It doesn't have to say you are absolutely the world's best at something, just kind words about you, your work and your performance. If a team member says thanks for taking the time to listen – that goes in there. If the CEO says that project was handled well – that goes in there. Just build up your evidence that you are great at what you do.

When you put these steps into action and do them consistently, you will find that the voice of your former bullying boss comes up less often and has much less impact on you. If you've experienced bullying, harassment or discrimination, it can help to talk to others who understand. I've listed some organizations at the end of the book which could help.

How do I keep myself motivated in challenging times?

"I'm meant to be motivating my team but the last 12 months have been so hard I often don't want to get out of bed on Monday morning and tackle my to-do list. How do I keep myself motivated in challenging times?"

Leaders are not robots and we do have fluctuating energy levels, moments of feeling unmotivated and a wide range of emotions. As leaders we can expend so much energy motivating our team that we have none left for ourselves.

To help keep yourself motivated, it's useful to understand why you're feeling demotivated and then problem solve from there.

Some things that can cause us to be demotivated:

1. You could be burnt out

We only have so much physical, mental and emotional energy and in challenging times we use up a lot of that just getting through the working day. If you think of it like a battery, your battery could be running very low and need recharging.

2. Your work or organization may be misaligned with your values

When you feel like your values aren't being respected, it can really impact your motivation.

Jane is a member of Influence & Impact who works in education and one of her core values is around making impact. She's a change maker and making a positive difference by improving things really lights her up. She was really struggling with her motivation because she'd joined a new organization at a time when COVID-19 restrictions meant the organization had zero appetite for change or improvements in her area. It just wasn't a priority for her employer. She felt unable to add real value and like she was being forced to settle for the inadequate status quo.

When we identified that it was this lack of impact that was demotivating Jane, I asked her to think of other ways she could make an impact, whether within work or outside of it. She came up with a few ideas and felt like she was back on track again.

The first step is knowing your values; then if you realize your values are feeling misaligned you can take action to change that.

3. You may have an unhelpful story about work

By now you know I'm big on identifying and reframing any unhelpful stories you have about work. So note the thoughts you have which make you feel less motivated. They might be about not feeling valued or appreciated by colleagues, not being good enough at your job or having so much to do you feel overwhelmed. Then head over to the coaching tool in Chapter 2 on reframing unhelpful beliefs to find a story that will motivate you.

And here are some other techniques you can try to increase your motivation:

A quote I find comforting during tough times is *"This too shall pass."* Everything is constantly changing and while it might seem like work has been challenging forever, actually there are moments of brightness.

Remind yourself of your *why*. Think back to what motivated you to take this job. Even if within your particular job you're not able to get the satisfaction that you would normally get from working on your *why*, perhaps you can think long term and focus on how you are still working for an organization you believe in, or still have a great team or are financially supporting your family.

Sometimes a lack of motivation can come from feeling like we are not succeeding or making progress. So have a chat to your manager and get clarity on what is expected of you and some feedback on your performance. If your manager isn't available to do that, try reflecting on your progress using the Leadership Wheel tool in Chapter 8.

Celebrate the small wins because that feeling of making progress will really give you a boost of energy – help your team to celebrate the small wins as well. And find the areas where you can make progress. So maybe you can't do the big picture progress or impact that you actually wanted to do. But what are the areas where you can make some progress?

You could keep a weekly achievements list where you write down what you've done. I know often I can spend all day on email, and it feels like I haven't achieved anything. But actually I have; I've been moving things forward. And so that achievements list helps me to recognize that and also recognize my own good attributes.

Another motivation boosting list is a gratitude list – it's been proven to boost your mental and physical health to reflect daily on what you are grateful for and it will shift your energy from looking at the negatives to seeing the positives.

Recognize that motivation isn't a constant. We were not designed to operate at full speed constantly. Get to know the ebbs and flows of your energy and motivation during your working day so that you can do the work that really needs you to be energized and motivated when that is how you are feeling.

> *"I noticed that by 4pm all I want to do is eat chocolate and nap. Now I manage my day so that I have my important meetings and tasks earlier in the day and can do the mindless admin from 4pm onwards. It has really helped my productivity." Karen*

In the short term you can also shift your state to boost your mood. You can do this quickly by listening to a song you love, going for a brisk walk, dancing, doing a few jumping jacks or just remembering a moment of success.

Finally, know that it is okay to feel demotivated sometimes. Yes, as a manager or leader part of our role is to motivate our team. But we are also human. And we're allowed to be honest about that. I think authenticity is really important. It builds trust and rapport.

How can I build my credibility as a young manager?

"I'm younger than most people at my level and those I manage and I worry that they don't take me seriously."

I struggled with this issue too as a young director – most people at my level were at least ten years older than me. But I realized that while I couldn't do much to change their first impressions of me, I could quickly gain their respect because I knew what I was talking about.

The first thing to bear in mind is that you are not a mind reader and not everyone is looking at you and doubting your credibility. Most people probably admire your success or feel like an underachiever next to you.

When it comes to meeting new people you want to start strong. If you're leading the meeting then get it off to a good start by taking control so that people are not looking to someone older to do that. If you're an attendee, try and speak early and use the tips in Chapter 5 to ensure that you are starting and finishing your contributions with clarity and confidence. Ask intelligent questions and basically show rather than tell that you know your stuff.

Owning a point of difference is better than pretending it doesn't exist. Yes, you may be young but there are benefits to that – you might bring energy, a fresh perspective, highly relevant experience, and so on. Get clear on why you were hired and own those reasons. You can also name the elephant in the room if you feel it is an issue by acknowledging that you are young but you have relevant expertise. I often used to do this in a lighthearted way which diffused the tension.

When it comes to the people you manage, you can apply many of the tools and concepts within Part 2 about being seen as a leader. Your Cloak of Authority will help you have the difficult conversations, your Personal Leadership Brand will help you be intentional about how you want to be perceived, and many of the suggestions about being promoted above your peers in Chapter 9 also apply here.

How can I influence when working virtually?

"I am struggling to influence internally now that we are working virtually as I don't have access to people in the same way. I used to chat to them after meetings but now we all just log off."

This topic has come up a lot within my Influence & Impact course so I've crowdsourced some tips on what's been working for members.

- **Communicate what you're doing with monthly reports** – this is a tool that works really well for influencing as you can share what your team is working on (encouraging collaboration) and can also make specific requests and thank colleagues who are helping you achieve your goals (building social capital). Make it a succinct and interesting read and share it with peers and relevant senior stakeholders to increase the visibility of your team.

- **Use social media** – I picked this tip up from the book *The Social CEO*, which shared examples of how leaders were celebrating colleagues and sharing their expertise on social media, using LinkedIn and Twitter in particular.[1] You can follow the people you want to influence (internal and external), engage with their content, celebrate team achievements and share your expertise in posts and tweets.

- **Improve on Zoom** – there is a lot you can do to make a better impression when engaging in online meetings or presenting. Make sure your background is professional if possible (or has something interesting that sparks conversation), that you are well framed in the camera, your lighting is decent and that you are using the chat box to engage and ask questions and share useful resources. You can also then follow up with those resources afterwards as no-one remembers to save their chat.

- **Dial up your energy** – our energy can get diluted through Zoom or Teams so it is worth consciously dialing up your energy so that you are seen. That looks different for each of us – it might be about body language or movement, varying your tone of voice or pace of speaking, or just thinking to yourself *"I want to be high energy."*

- **Checking in** – you can always drop someone an email asking how they are or how that project they are working on is going. We might do that for our team but it is rare to do it for someone more senior than you; it shows interest in their work and wellbeing.

- **Ask for a quick call** – if you have a specific topic in mind, you can still ask for a quick call with a stakeholder to get their input. Explain what you need and why and by when. If you can't get a call, you could record a short video or voice message explaining the key points if you prefer that to an email.

How do I deal with tension between my team and another team?

"I am constantly getting dragged into the detail of discussions between my team and another team as they can't resolve it between themselves and it is such a waste of my time."

There are a few angles you can take with this:

- **You can coach your team** – I would start by exploring the narrative that they have around this other team as once we decide another team is hard to deal with then we think everything they do is unhelpful. You can take them through the perspectives coaching exercise in Chapter 6 and get them to see the situation from the other team's point of view. You can also coach them on their problem-solving skills, influencing skills and be clear on the authority that they have and what it is appropriate and not appropriate to involve you in. If there is a head of team in place then I would also talk to them about your expectations of them at this level when it comes to working with peers and cross-departmentally.
- **You can meet with your peer in the other team** – follow the advice in Chapter 6 and have a meeting which identifies the issues and causes. Together (potentially with your teams too) you can co-create a

new and better way of working, having addressed the
problems head on.

- **Seek clarity** – often tensions arise over a lack of
  clarity when it comes to responsibility, authority or
  expectations. If you and your peer can't resolve this
  together, you can seek clarity from your own manager
  (and theirs) about the area in which the issue is
  arising. This is your final port of call if the other two
  approaches don't solve the issue as otherwise you are
  just pushing the issue upwards without contributing
  to a solution.

How do I stop my team constantly asking me questions?

"I seem to spend all my time answering my team's questions and not focusing on my own priorities. It's exhausting and never seems to get better. What can I do?"

One of the unspoken myths of management is that we have to be constantly available to our team and it is an unhelpful one. In fact, being constantly available could be holding them back rather than helping them. It is a bit like spoon feeding your young child – yes, it is quicker and less messy then letting them do it themselves but if you keep doing it they never learn the skill of feeding themselves.

Many of us have a desire to be helpful and solve problems for our team but if we overdo that they learn that it is quicker to ask you a question than find out the answer for themselves. And who doesn't want to do things the quick and easy way? We are constantly training people how to treat us by our behavior and what we allow, and you've trained your team to rely on you rather than think for themselves.

If you'd like to press the reset button on how often your team come to you for answers, here are some steps you can take:

- **Stop answering their questions and instead ask "*What do you think?*", "*What have you come up with so far?*" or "*What have you considered as options?*".** At first, they will be a bit perplexed that you are asking them to think for themselves but then they will learn to expect that question, will ask it of themselves and will often come up with answer without needing to ask you.

- **Check that they have the authority and expertise they need to come up with their own answers** – are they worried that they won't do it right or are they being tasked with work they are not trained to do? It's also worth checking in with yourself on both your delegation skills (see Chapter 4) and that you're not a secret control freak who they're scared of upsetting.

- **Help them build their confidence** as that can sometimes be an issue, along with a fear of failure; a course around confidence and assertiveness can help with that. Check out my website for courses like that.

- **Notice repetitive questions and create a system** where they know where to find the answers. They will soon get bored of you saying "*Have you looked on the system?*"

How do I improve my relationship with my manager?

"My manager and I are very different and we seem to clash often. I'm worried this is going to damage my career."

Tension between a manager and one of their reports isn't unusual. After all, there are plenty of reasons for that tension, including different management style preferences, communication styles, priorities and personalities. But it is an important relationship to get right if you want to progress within your organization.

The biggest step you can take is to try and see the issue as being about the dynamic between the two of you – not their fault or your fault. If you can depersonalize it like this then you are more likely to be able to respond rather than react when you interact with each other. You will also be able to have a bit more perspective and identify where you may be contributing to the tension.

If your manager is questioning the *way* you do things, it is worth understanding what they are worried about and what they want you to achieve. Take those concerns seriously – they may well be valid and you may need to take on board what they are saying and do things a bit differently. Or you may feel that you do things in a different way but one which is equally valid. After reflecting on that, you can then communicate to your manager that you understand their concerns, that the two of you are aligned on what you are trying to achieve, and that you believe your approach is simply an alternative way to do it.

Different communication and thinking styles can also be a source of tension. Introverts can feel pressured to provide answers on the spot in meetings, while extroverts can feel frustrated at the lack of immediate input they receive. Some of us are highly detailed and others only want to look at the big picture. I always advise understanding your manager's preferences and communicating in a way that will land with them. You can literally speak their language by using phrases that they use. Often the issue isn't what you are saying but instead the language you are using or how you are presenting it. There are some good frameworks for this in Chapter 7 on speaking the language of senior stakeholders.

How do I deal with professional jealousy?

"When I see people being promoted around me, I feel jealous and can't help wondering why I am not being given that opportunity. I don't feel like they are better performers than I am."

Let's look at what's going on inside you first. Jealousy is an unedited pang of emotion prompted by the fact someone has what we want. It can be a useful reminder that something is important to us – in this situation, it may be that you would like to be promoted or it could be that you'd like more acknowledgment of the value you add to the organization. So my first suggestion is to ask yourself *"what is this jealousy telling me?"* and see what comes up for you.

As with any emotion, try and accept and embrace it rather than shame yourself for it and it will pass quicker. So be kind to yourself – feeling jealous or comparing others unfavorably to yourself is perfectly normal and doesn't make you a bad person.

There may be circumstantial reasons why you've not been promoted. As women we do face additional barriers to being seen as credible when men are making decisions because, being human, they are drawn to people they can easily relate to. We have to work harder to prove our credibility and women progress more slowly than men due to gender bias. This impacts women of color even more significantly due to systemic racism.[1]

If you are ready for a promotion then there are steps you can take to close the Influence Gap and make that more likely. The good news is that if you've read this book and Part 4 in particular, and are implementing it, you are now on a pathway toward that. Review your Personal Leadership Brand to see if that needs tweaking. If you've thought about what sort of attributes and skills are celebrated and valued by your employer, if those don't align with what you bring or what is important to you, that could be a reason you've not been recognized.

Most importantly, have the conversation with your manager about your career goals and seek feedback on why you've not been put forward for new opportunities. They may well think you are very happy at your current level or they may have some useful feedback. Putting your ambitions on their radar gives them the opportunity to help you achieve them.

How do I say no?

"I find it hard to say no to my colleagues and manager and as a result I am overworked, overwhelmed and increasingly frustrated."

There are many reasons why we find it hard to say no. Some of us are people pleasers and have an emotional desire to please others at the expense of our own needs and desires. Sometimes we don't know how to say no without causing tension. Sometimes we've tried to say no and been ignored so we've given up. Unfortunately, if we keep saying yes to everything it can be a fast track to burnout.

If you think you might be a people pleaser, there are a few things you can do about that. First, identify what you believe will happen if you stop saying yes and run that belief through the reframing beliefs exercise in Chapter 2. Second, I want you to get very clear on what it is costing you to say yes. And finally think about what you want, as it can be easy to lose that when you are focused on the needs of other people. What do you want and who can you ask for that?

If you find it hard to say no because you don't know how to do it, here are some tips:

- Have clear written priorities to refer to so that if someone asks you to do something outside of those priorities, you can simply say, *"I have to remain focused on those priorities."*
- Make sure you have clarity on your roles and responsibilities – often we can end up saying yes to things

that we don't believe are within our job remit because the person asking has a strong personality. If you don't think something is within your remit then get clarity on that from your manager; find out where it does sit so you can push back with confidence.

- Communicate to your colleagues and manager that you don't have the capacity to take on anymore work at this point in time.
- If the work is coming from your manager, try saying "This sounds like a great project. I'm at full capacity at the moment; if this is a priority, what would you like me to stop doing or reallocate to someone else?"
- Use your Cloak of Authority to help you feel confident having those conversations.

In Chapter 4 on leading your team you'll also find some useful insights on how you can overcome a fear of difficult conversations and how to set clear boundaries.

Conclusion

My hope is that this book will sit on your desk as a practical resource that you can draw on when you need it. There is no need to apply everything you've learned immediately – just choose the first thing, give it a try and it if helps you keep doing it. Then do the same again the following week. As leaders we never arrive at the finish line; we are constantly learning, evolving and adapting, particularly as we step into new roles or move into new organizations.

And remember – you are not alone, there is nothing wrong with you and by leading your way you can help to change the workplace, one interaction at a time.

If you've found this book helpful, I'd love to hear about it – you can connect with me on LinkedIn, leave a review on Amazon or drop me a message on my website. It makes my day to know I've made a positive difference to someone.

Want to dive deeper with me?

Influence & Impact is my 12-month group coaching course for female leaders. Hundreds of women have gone through the course which includes:

- Bite-sized modules diving deeper into the topics explored in this book.

- A monthly teaching call to connect with the other incredible women in the group.
- A monthly coaching clinic where you can be coached by me.
- A private Facebook community for advice, support and encouragement.
- The opportunity to be part of a supportive and inspiring network of successful women.

"Carla's 12-month programme has undoubtedly been the best investment I have made to my career development to date. She strikes the perfect balance between humanizing leadership, including promoting emotional literacy as a core component of leading with confidence, and practical, clear advice and tools to empower you to be your best professional self. I self-funded and it felt like a gamble at the start, but those worries quickly subsided – the growth I have experienced has been absolutely worth it. I feel so much more comfortable in my skin, feel able to step forward and take radical responsibility and have very solid influencing skills. My confidence has skyrocketed and instead of feeling 'I can't' or feeling like a bit of an imposter I feel like I CAN – and if things don't go perfectly that's simply something to grow and learn from. I know now what I want my future to look like and the kind of career I want to build, based on my values and what I do best. It has been a great experience, in sum, and I thoroughly recommend working with Carla". Anna, Change Lead (who went on to secure a huge promotion)

"I joined Influence & Impact when I was looking for professional and personal development in the leadership space.

I am so grateful for the fantastic community of women leaders I was able to meet through Carla's programme, joining many Zoom calls, having access to an online portal which is full of extremely insightful and helpful resources to help me become a more confident and knowledgeable leader. Influence & Impact also helped me navigate redundancy and find an amazing new job I love (thanks to interview tips I picked up on her online portal). I therefore highly recommend her programmes and podcast series which touch on important topics that help mid-senior managers grow in their roles." Marion, project manager (who secured a brilliant new job after redundancy)

Visit my website **www.carlamillertraining.com** to find out more about Influence & Impact, and the other ways I can support you and your organization.

Notes

Introduction

[1] Darina L., "Shocking male vs female CEO statistics 2022," 6 March 2020. Available from https://leftronic.com/blog/ceo-statistics/ [accessed April 28, 2022].

[2] Goldman Sachs, "Launch with GS." Available from www.goldmansachs.com/our-commitments/diversity-and-inclusion/launch-with-gs/ [accessed April 28, 2022].

[3] SVB Financial Group, *Women in Technology Leadership 2019: Key Insights from the Silicon Valley Bank Startup Outlook Survey*, 2019. Available from www.svb.com/globalassets/library/uploadedfiles/content/trends_and_insights/reports/women_in_technology_leadership/svb-suo-women-in-tech-report-2019.pdf [accessed April 28, 2022].

[4] World Economic Forum, *Global Gender Gap Report 2021: Insight Report*, 2021. Available from www.weforum.org/reports/global-gender-gap-report-2021/digest [accessed April 28, 2022].

[5] A.H. Eagly, S.J. Karau, & M.G. Makhijani (1995). "Gender and the effectiveness of leaders: A meta-analysis." *Psychological Bulletin*, 117, 125–145.

[6] Naomi Cahn, "Women's status and pay in the C-Suite." *Forbes*, February 19, 2021. Available from www.forbes.com/sites/naomicahn/2021/02/19/womens-status-and-pay-in-the-c-suite--new-study/?sh=27d5f21e3762 [accessed April 28, 2022].

[7] Loughborough University, "Women are given feedback that is likely to slow down their progression to senior roles, new research finds," October 8, 2019. Available from www.lboro.ac.uk/

news-events/news/2019/october/womens-feedback-likely-to-slow-down-their-progress/ [accessed April 28, 2022].

[8] Samantha C. Paustian-Underdahl, Lisa Slattery Walker, & David J. Woehr (2014). "Gender and perceptions of leadership effectiveness: A meta-analysis of contextual moderators." *Journal of Applied Psychology*, 99(6), 1129–1145. https://doi.apa.org/doi/10.1037/a0036751

[9] H. Ibarra, R.J. Ely, & D.M. Kolb, "Women rising: The unseen barriers," *Harvard Business Review*, September 2013. Available from https://hbr.org/2013/09/women-rising-the-unseen-barriers [accessed April 28, 2022].

[10] Employers Network for Equality & Inclusion, "Women less comfortable making their voices heard at work," September 12, 2017. Available from https://enei.org.uk/resources/news/women-less-comfortable-making-their-voices-heard-at-work/ [accessed April 28, 2022].

[11] Victoria L. Brescoll, "Who takes the floor and why: Gender, power and volubility in organizations." Harvard Kennedy School, 2012. Available from https://gap.hks.harvard.edu/who-takes-floor-and-why-gender-power-and-volubility-organizations [accessed April 28, 2022].

[12] Deborah Tannen, "The truth about how much women talk — and whether men listen." *Time*, June 28, 2017. Available from https://time.com/4837536/do-women-really-talk-more/ [accessed April 28, 2022].

[13] Natalie Baumgartner, "Women don't feel they belong in the workplace." *The HR Director*, September 13, 2021. Available from www.thehrdirector.com/business-news/employee-engagement/women-dont-feel-they-belong-in-the-workplace-global-survey-finds/ [accessed April 28, 2022].

[14] McKinsey & Company, *Women in the Workplace 2020*. Available from https://wiw-report.s3.amazonaws.com/Women_in_the_Workplace_2020.pdf [accessed April 28, 2022].

[15] McKinsey & Company, "Women in the Workplace 2021," September 27, 2021. Available from www.mckinsey.com/featured-insights/diversity-and-inclusion/women-in-the-workplace [accessed April 28, 2022].

Chapter 1

[1] For a full reference list on the imposter phenomenon, see Pauline R. Clance, "Imposter Phenomenon (IP)," 2013. Available from https://paulineroseclance.com/impostor_phenomenon.html [accessed April 28, 2022].

[2] Elizabeth Gilbert, *Big Magic: How to Live a Creative Life, and Let Go of Your Fear*. Bloomsbury, 2015.

[3] Elizabeth R. Thornton, *The Objective Leader: How to Leverage the Power of Seeing Things as They Are*. St Martin's Press, 2015.

[4] Brittney Saline, "4 ways to stop relying on external validation." *Talkspace*, August 5, 2019. Available from www.talkspace.com/blog/validation-opinions-stop-seeking/ [accessed April 28, 2022].

[5] Louise Hay, *You Can Heal Your Life*. Hay House, 1984.

Chapter 2

[1] Carol Dweck, *Mindset: Changing the Way you Think to Fulfil Your Potential*. Robinson, 2017.

[2] Byron Katie, *Loving What Is: Four Questions That Can Change Your Life*. Rider, 2002.

Chapter 3

[1] Ben Wigert, "Employee burnout: The biggest myth." *Gallup*, March 13, 2020. Available from www.gallup.com/workplace/288539/employee-burnout-biggest-myth.aspx [accessed April 28, 2022].

[2] Jessica Stillman, "The 12 stages of burnout, according to psychologists." *Inc.*, August 2, 2017. Available from www.inc.com/jessica-stillman/the-12-stages-of-burnout-according-to-psychologist.html [accessed April 28, 2022].

[3] Stephen Covey, *The 7 Habits of Highly Effective People*. 30th Anniversary edition. Simon & Schuster, 2020.

[4] Oprah, "Shonda Rhimes' touching message for her daughters," 15 November 2015. Available from www.oprah.com/own-super-soul-sunday/shonda-rhimes-touching-message-for-her-daughters-video [accessed April 28, 2022].

[5] Paul Gilbert, *The Compassionate Mind*. Constable, 2010.

[6] Teresa Amabile and Steven Kramer, *The Progress Principle: Using Small Wins to Ignite Joy, Engagement, and Creativity at Work*. Harvard Business Review Press, 2011.

[7] Carol Dweck, *Mindset: Changing the Way You Think to Fulfil Your Potential*. Robinson, 2017.

Chapter 4

[1] Catherine Moore, "Positive daily affirmations: Is there science behind it?" *PositivePsychology.com*, March 24, 2022. Available from https://positivepsychology.com/daily-affirmations/ [accessed April 28, 2022].

[2] Brené Brown, *The Gifts of Imperfection*. Vermilion, 2020, p. 19.

[3] Martin Zwilling, "How to delegate more effectively in your business". *Forbes*, October 2, 2013. Available from www.forbes.com/sites/martinzwilling/2013/10/02/how-to-delegate-more-effectively-in-your-business/?sh=68f085be69bc [accessed April 28, 2022].

Chapter 5

[1] McKinsey & Company, *Women in the Workplace 2019*. Available from www.mckinsey.com/~/media/McKinsey/Featured%20Insights/Gender%20Equality/Women%20in%20the%20Workplace%202019/Women-in-the-workplace-2019.ashx [accessed April 28, 2022].

[2] TEDGlobal 2012, "Your body language may shape who you are," June 2012. Available from www.ted.com/talks/amy_cuddy_your_body_language_may_shape_who_you_are/transcript?language=en [accessed April 28, 2022].

[3] Juliet Eilperin, "White House women want to be in the room where it happens." *The Washington Post*, September 13, 2016. Available from www.washingtonpost.com/news/powerpost/wp/2016/09/13/white-house-women-are-now-in-the-room-where-it-happens/ [accessed April 28, 2022].

[4] Valerie Rein, *Patriarchy Stress Disorder: The Invisible Inner Barrier to Women's Happiness and Fulfillment*. Lioncrest Publishing, 2019.

[5] Caroline Goyder, *Gravitas: Communicate with Confidence, Influence and Authority*. Vermilion, 2014, p. 87.

[6] Caroline Goyder, *Gravitas: Communicate with Confidence, Influence and Authority*. Vermilion, 2014, pp. 88–89.

Chapter 6

[1] Jill Bolte-Taylor, *My Stroke of Insight: A Brain Scientist's Personal Journey*. Hodder & Stoughton, 2008.

Chapter 7

[1] Deloitte, "The Deloitte Millennial Survey 2018." Available from www2.deloitte.com/tr/en/pages/about-deloitte/articles/millennialsurvey-2018.html [accessed April 28, 2022].

Chapter 8

[1] Helen Tupper and Sarah Ellis, *The Squiggly Career: Ditch the Ladder, Discover Opportunity, Design Your Career*. Portfolio Penguin, 2020.

[2] See www.carlamillertraining.com

[3] BBC News, "Gender pay gap 'at risk of worsening', says campaigners," November 7, 2012. Available from www.bbc.co.uk/news/business-20223264 [accessed April 28, 2022].

[4] Gill Whitty-Collins, *Why Men Win at Work …and How We Can Make Inequality History*. Luath Press, 2020, p. 99.

How to do I recover for a bullying boss?

[1] Allie Caren, "Why we often remember the bad better than the good." *The Washington Post*, November 1, 2018. Available from www.washingtonpost.com/science/2018/11/01/why-we-often-remember-bad-better-than-good/ [accessed April 28, 2022].

How can I influence when working virtually?

[1] Damian Corbet, *The Social CEO: How Social Media Can Make You a Stronger Leader*. Bloomsbury, 2019.

How do I deal with professional jealousy?

[1] There is much evidence on these points in Gill Whitty-Collins, *Why Men Win at Work … and How We Can Make Inequality History*. Luath Press, 2020.

Resources and further reading

You can listen to my podcast, *Influence & Impact for Female Leaders*, on all major podcast platforms for interviews on many of the topics I discuss in this book.

Further reading

Bolte-Taylor, Jill. 2008. *My Stroke of Insight: A Brain Scientist's Personal Journey*. Hodder & Stoughton.

Brown, Brené. 2020. *The Gifts of Imperfection*. Vermilion.

Cuddy, Amy. 2015. *Presence: Bringing Your Boldest Self to Your Biggest Challenges*. Orion.

Goyder, Caroline. 2014. *Gravitas: Communicate with Confidence, Influence and Authority*. Vermilion.

Grant, Adam. 2021. *Think Again: The Power of Knowing What You Don't Know*. WH Allen.

Mahdawi, Arwa. 2021. *Strong Female Lead: Rethinking Leadership in a World Gone Wrong*. Hodder & Stoughton.

Sieghart, Mary Ann. 2021. *The Authority Gap: Why Women Are Still Taken Less Seriously Than Men, and What We Can Do About It*. Transworld.

Sword-Williams, Stefanie. 2020. *F*ck Being Humble: Why Self-Promotion Isn't a Dirty Word*. Quadrille.

Whitty-Collins, Gill. 2020. *Why Men Win at Work … and How We Can Make Inequality History*. Luath Press.

Young, Valerie. 2011. *The Secret Thoughts of Successful Women: Why Capable People Suffer from the Impostor Syndrome and How to Thrive in Spite of It*. Crown Business.

These are just some of the brilliant women I know supporting women in a variety of ways – go follow them on Instagram or LinkedIn:

@TheJobSharePair for job sharing inspiration and consultancy
@Anotheredoor for redundancy support
@Worklifemother for scaling the maternal wall
@Comebackcommunity for returning to the workplace after a break
@WOCGN Women of Colour Global Network
@tryingyears for fertility and the workplace
@henpicked for menopause support
@Pregnant_then_screwed for the rights of working mums

Relevant helplines, campaigning and support organizations

@speak_out_revolution for workplace harassment and bullying
@pregnant_then_screwed for ending the motherhood penalty and maternity discrimination
Mind and Samaritans helplines for mental health

Acknowledgments

Thank you to all the women who have trusted me as their coach over the past decade, and in particular the incredible members of the Influence & Impact community, many of whom funded themselves, and who inspire me every day with their wisdom, encouragement and courage. Your experiences are helping others through this book. Doing my job is a privilege and one I don't take lightly.

Thank you to the organizations that have hired me to speak to and work with their female employees – it is so encouraging to witness your commitment to tackling gender equality.

I have learned so much from the many wonderful guests on my Influence & Impact podcast and made friends along the way. And I am grateful to everyone who listens weekly – your messages about the impact it has made on you make my day.

Thank you to my wonderful team, Karen Richie, Tahirih McLaren-Brown and Steve Campden, who do all the things I'm not very good at so I can spend my time coaching, podcasting and writing this book. And also the fantastic associate coaches Jennifer McCanna and Haseena Farid who co-lead workshops with me and help create the safe space for women to share openly.

The illustrations in this book were created by the talented Liam Williams of LeoDo.

Thank you to those who kindly read and endorsed this book – all very talented and respected individuals who generously supported me. And to my lovely beta reader Emma-Louise Singh for her support and generally being a great cheerleader.

A huge thank you to everyone involved in the production, publication and marketing of this book led by the wise and wonderful Alison Jones of Practical Inspiration.

And my biggest thank you goes to my family for supporting me as both a solo mum and a business owner. You have always believed in me and given me the support I needed to create this life I am lucky enough to lead. And, of course, to my little boy Charlie, who reminds me that there is more to life than work and makes me laugh every day.

About the author

Carla Miller is a leadership coach and keynote speaker who works with women to develop their careers and their confidence. She also supports employers to develop and retain their female talent, build their pipeline of female leaders and encourage male allyship. Hundreds of women leaders have taken part in her Influence & Impact course from companies including GSK, BT, Channel 4, Muller and Deloitte, as well as national charities, the NHS and the Civil Service.

Carla's own leadership experience includes raising £20 million for good causes and leading the fundraising at Samaritans and many other national charities; she was CEO of Tiny Tickers and then managing director of Charity People, a leading charity recruitment consultancy alongside founding her own coaching business.

She hosts the chart-topping Influence & Impact podcast for female leaders, which has featured leading thinkers such as Graham Allcott, Harriet Minter and Stefanie Sword-Williams. Carla has also featured in national media such as *The Guardian* and *Psychologies* magazine and regularly chairs conference panels on leadership.

When she's not working, Carla is a solo parent to her little boy and can be found on countryside walks or building Lego.

Index